D1400303

The Sacred Text

Princeton Theological Monograph Series

K. C. Hanson and Charles M. Collier, Series Editors

Recent volumes in the series:

Catherine L. Kelsey
*Schleiermacher's Preaching, Dogmatics, and Biblical Criticism:
The Interpretation of Jesus Christ in the Gospel of John*

Christian T. Collins Winn, editor
*From the Margins: A Celebration of the Theological Work
of Donald W. Dayton*

Gabriel Andrew Msoka
*Basic Human Rights and the Humanitarian Crises
in Sub-Saharan Africa: Ethical Reflections*

T. David Beck
*The Holy Spirit and the Renewal of All Things:
Pneumatology in Paul and Jurgen Moltmann*

Trevor Dobbs
*Faith, Theology, and Psychoanalysis:
The Life and Thought of Harry S. Guntrip*

Paul S. Chung, Kim Kyoung-Jae, and Veli-Matti Kärkkäinen, editors
*Asian Contextual Theology for the Third Millennium:
A Theology of Minjung in Fourth-Eye Formation*

Bonnie L. Pattison
Poverty in the Theology of John Calvin

Anette Ejsing
A Theology of Anticipation: A Constructive Study of C. S. Peirce

Michael G. Cartwright
*Practices, Politics, and Performance: Toward a Communal
Hermeneutic for Christian Ethics*

Stephen Finlan and Vladimir Kharlamov, editors
Theōsis: Deification in Christian Theology

The Sacred Text

Biblical Authority in Nineteenth-Century America

Ronald F. Satta

Pickwick *Publications*

An imprint of *Wipf and Stock Publishers*
199 West 8th Avenue • Eugene OR 97401

ISBN 13: 978-1-55635-298-0

Cataloging-in-Publication data:

Satta, Ronald F.

The sacred text : biblical authority in nineteenth-century America / Ronald F. Satta.

Eugene, Ore.: Pickwick Publications, 2007
Princeton Theological Monograph Series 73

xvi + 116 p. ; 23 cm.

Includes bibliography

ISBN 13: 978-1-55635-298-0

1. Bible—Evidences, authority, etc. 2. Princeton Theological Seminary—History. 3. Briggs, Charles A. (Charles Augustus), 1841–1913—Trials, litigation, etc. I. Title. II. Series.

BS480 .S27 2007

This book is dedicated to those I love most—
who make life happy—
my family.

Contents

Introduction

NINETEENTH-CENTURY American Protestants revered the Bible as a special book. Scripture occupied a prominent place in their religious, intellectual, and social life. Not least of those preoccupied with the Bible were those few charged with interpreting and conveying its message.

What did these theological elites believe about the Bible? In precisely what way was it special to them? Did nineteenth-century Protestant theologians possess a coherent, well-defined doctrine of biblical authority—and if so what was it? Did a consensus exist among Presbyterians, Baptists, Congregationalists, Methodists, and other Protestant scholars and religious leaders or is there evidence of disagreement along denominational lines? If variation existed, what were the parameters of the debate? What similarities and disparities existed among and between them?

What influence did the emerging science of geology, the rise of Darwinism, and higher text critical theories have on the doctrine of Scripture in America? When Protestant elite spoke of Scripture as inspired what did they mean precisely—was it a general notion pertaining only to the ideas expressed in the Bible or a more technical doctrine encompassing the actual words? Did they consider the sacred text reliable only for faith and religious practice or did its authority extend to issues pertaining to history and science as well? These questions are of added importance because of a recent controversy regarding biblical authority. An important tenet endorsed by American fundamentalists is the doctrine of biblical inerrancy. As one historian has observed, "A firm trust and belief in every word of the Bible . . . has been both the pride and the scandal of Fundamentalism."[1]

American Fundamentalists and many evangelicals believe that inerrancy represents the traditional orthodox opinion of both the ancient and Reformation Church.[2] Furthermore, they contend that a belief in an er-

---

1. Sandeen, *Roots of Fundamentalism*, 3.

2. The term "Evangelical" is quite broad, including a range of Protestant groups. Three major doctrinal strands unite this otherwise disparate ecclesiastical conglomerate: (1) a commitment to Scriptural authority, (2) the belief in the need for regeneration through faith in Christ alone, and (3) a desire to participate in the propagation of the gospel.

rorless Bible long represented the dominant opinion in the United States and elsewhere. In contrast, some influential modern scholars of American religion argue that the doctrine of inerrancy is a recent, late nineteenth-century innovation, a misguided addendum to Protestant theology. For instance, in his important book *The Roots of Fundamentalism*, Ernest Sandeen argues that a well-defined doctrine of Scripture, including inerrancy of the original autographs, did not exist prior to 1881.[3]

Sandeen accuses two Princeton scholars of theological duplicity by concocting the doctrine of inerrancy in an influential article entitled "Inspiration," which appeared in the *Presbyterian Review* in 1881. In this article A. A. Hodge and B. B. Warfield stoutly defended the errorless quality of the first-edition canonical text as it came fresh from the hands of the sacred penmen—the original autographs. Everything Scripture teaches, they urged, whether regarding matters of faith or fact is completely reliable—right down to the precise words of the autographs.

Challenged by higher critics and geological science, these two scholars purportedly fabricated the doctrine in an effort to insulate Scripture from assault, making it impervious to criticism.[4] Arguing that a well-defined doctrine of biblical authority which included inerrancy did not exist prior to the Hodge and Warfield article, Sandeen asserts:

> A systematic theology of biblical authority which defended the common Evangelical faith in the infallibility of the Bible had to be created in the midst of the nineteenth-century controversy. The formation of this theory in association with the growth of the millenarian movement determined the character of Fundamentalism.[5]

Thus fundamentalists, Sandeen contends, wrongly embraced inerrancy, believing that in doing so they were allied with the traditional Protestant theory of inspiration, when in fact they had been deceived by a recent innovation.

Sandeen specifically states the artifice of which he accuses Hodge and Warfield. It included teaching that (1) inspiration extended to the very words of Scripture; (2) the Scriptures taught their own inerrancy; and (3) inspiration extended only to the original autographs.[6] If his case is sound,

---

Though some progressive evangelicals reject biblical inerrancy, many classical evangelicals, like their fundamentalist brethren, endorse it. For a further discussion on Evangelicalism, see Dayton and Johnson, *Variety of American Evangelicalism*, 1991.

3. Sandeen, *Roots of Fundamentalism*, 127–28.

4. Ibid.

5. Ibid., 106.

6. Ibid., 123, 125, 127–28.

one would not expect to find earlier nineteenth-century Protestant theologians, biblical scholars, or religious leaders advancing such views in any clear and systematic manner. But, if the evidence indicates that they did so, a revision of Sandeen's influential theory seems in order.

Significant studies of fundamentalism bear the marks of the Sandeen thesis. In his highly respected book, *Fundamentalism and American Culture*, George Marsden says:

> Fundamentalism was the outgrowth of the "millenarian" movement that developed in late nineteenth-century America. . . . According to Sandeen, these Bible teachers acquired from conservative Presbyterians at Princeton Theological Seminary the newly-defined dogma that the Bible was inerrant in every detail.[7]

In their award-winning-book, *The Authority and Interpretation of the Bible: An Historical Approach*, Jack Rogers and Donald McKim expand Sandeen's argument, asserting that inerrancy was a recent guise disguised as traditional orthodoxy by late nineteenth-century Princeton scholars.[8]

In an earlier work on biblical authority, Rogers echoes the Sandeen theory while censuring the Warfield and Hodge article. He writes, "Thus errorlessness was confined to the original (lost) manuscripts of the Bible. . . . Since the original texts were not available, Warfield seemed to have an unassailable apologetic stance."[9] Sandeen's text has thus proved pioneering in condemning inerrancy as an innovation.

Critics of inerrancy appear to be dealing with the crest of the wave—the alleged late nineteenth-century emergence of inerrancy and later twentieth-century developments within fundamentalism. This study focuses on the undercurrents which gave lift to and sustained the wave, investigating what nineteenth-century biblical scholars from a variety of denominational backgrounds believed and taught about Scripture.

The evidence of the archives provides an illuminating backdrop against which to assess the modern controversy—which as the archival record will reveal is not so recent after all. Most rebuttals of the critical argument have concentrated on the work of Princeton Theological Seminary. This is understandable since Sandeen himself places Princeton in the cross hairs

---

7. Marsden, *Fundamentalism and American Culture*, 3–4. Though Marsden does much to dispel some of the cruder stereotypes related to fundamentalism, he seems to believe that the movement is misled in its commitment to inerrancy as the historic position of the Church.

8. Rogers and McKim, *Authority and Interpretation of the Bible*, 246–47, 285, 346–58.

9. Rogers, "Church Doctrine of Biblical Authority," 39.

of his criticism.[10] However, they were certainly not solitary voices when it came to issues of biblical authority, inspiration, and inerrancy in America. What did leaders in some of the fastest growing denominations contribute to the question of biblical authority? How did Baptist scholars view the Bible? What about Methodists? How did their scholars explain biblical authority in the nineteenth-century—how did they define the doctrine of inspiration? Did Congregational theologians and religious leaders believe in inerrancy?

By assessing scholarly literature produced by many of the leading voices of Protestantism from a variety of different backgrounds a comprehensive portrait of the dominant and subordinate theories of biblical authority in nineteenth-century America emerges. Such an analysis also reveals whether the Princetonians were truly mavericks out of step with mainstream Christian orthodoxy or if that is a portrait foisted upon them by recent critics.

Fortunately the dialogue between biblical scholars, theologians, and religious leaders throughout the nineteenth-century on the issue of biblical authority is well documented. Many scores of articles on the subject in more than a dozen theological journals appeared during this period. Scholars regularly discussed the degree of biblical accuracy one should expect regarding matters of history, geology, geography, science, and alleged errors in the text. Indeed, the journal record is one of the most fertile areas for such an investigation because that is precisely where the theological elite debated the issue between and among themselves with some of their clearest and most persuasive arguments.

Furthermore, these journals represent several different denominational outlooks. For instance, articles in the *Biblical Repertory and Princeton Review*, and *Southern Presbyterian Review* help establish Presbyterian ideology while those appearing in *Christian Review* and *Freewill Baptist Quarterly* identify Baptist tendencies. The *Universalist Quarterly* and the *Methodist Magazine and Quarterly Review* obviously espouse their denominational perspective on the matter. Other journals, such as *Bibliotheca Sacra*, the

---

10 J.D. Woodbridge and R. H. Balmer have conducted incisive research into the doctrine of biblical authority endorsed by both Archibald Alexander and Charles Hodge. Their judicious analysis has resulted in a sturdy refutation of the Sandeen claim that inerrancy was a stranger to Princeton prior to the 1881 Hodge and Warfield article. I build upon their research, offering a broader assessment of biblical authority in nineteenth-century America. See Woodbridge and Balmer, "Princetonians and Biblical Authority," 251–79. I assess the claim that young Hodge and Warfield introduced the concept of inerrancy in their 1881 article "Inspiration" in the Appendix.

Theological and Literary Journal, and *Andover Review* invited participation from a diverse group of Protestant biblical scholars.

When the sacred text and the secular sciences seemed to contradict one another, how did Protestant theologians respond? When disagreements appeared unavoidable, which witness ultimately prevailed, Scripture or something else? Did theologians attempt to harmonize the secular and sacred accounts, thus protecting the integrity of the Bible or did they surrender its teaching to the voice of science? What sort of imbroglios did these theologians face in light of surging secular information?

A study of this sort is crucial for a number of reasons. First, it brings to light many of the important questions and controversies facing the elite throughout the century. The meteoric rise in secular knowledge exerted tremendous pressure on theologians of the time. Their ruminations, responses, quarrels, and convictions offer penetrating insight into their world—into their perspective on Scripture and authority and how their outlook was challenged, defended, and sometimes changed across time.

Second, it provides the most comprehensive framework with which to assess the modern argument condemning inerrancy and those who endorse it, creating an informed historical backdrop against which American fundamentalism may be critically reviewed. Are modern stereotypes relegating it to the intellectual and religious backwaters historically justified?[11] Furthermore, the evidence of this inquiry reveals the genesis from which the modern critical theory evolved.

Finally, a careful work on nineteenth-century biblical authority in America does not as yet exist. The highly regarded church historian, John Woodbridge, suggests that, "a detailed analysis of biblical authority in the nineteenth-century . . . still awaits its historian or historians."[12] This work is intended to partially fill that void, providing keener insight and greater clarity on the perceived role of the Bible in nineteenth-century America and the issue of biblical authority more broadly.

This brief introductory chapter has sketched the broad outline of those issues that will be explored and analyzed. Chapter one offers an examination of the doctrine of inspiration as understood by the Protestant

11. Fundamentalists are frequently stereotyped, at least partially, and perhaps principally, due to their doctrine of biblical authority. As Timothy Weber noted, "Many Americans equate fundamentalism with dogmatism, close-mindedness, right-wing politics, and the 'paranoid style.' To some extent these popular views have been encouraged by the conclusions of historians. Until fairly recently most historians have seen fundamentalism as a movement of the socially backward, intellectually stunted, theologically naïve, and psychologically disturbed." Weber, "Two-Edged Sword," 101.

12. Woodbridge and Balmer, "Princetonians," 278.

elite from about 1800–1860. It reveals the presence of a broad-based, clearly articulated, and staunchly defended endorsement of the doctrine of inerrancy. "High view" advocates believed that whether in matters of faith and practice, the discipline of history, the study of science, or the field of geography, Scripture served as the final arbiter.

Furthermore, the chapter also examines the Protestant commitment to the original autograph theory. Critics contend that the original manuscript doctrine originated in the late nineteenth-century at Princeton, representing the work of a few isolated theological loners. However, such an outlook is not sustained in the scholarship of the period.

Chapter two investigates the conservative response to growing criticism. "Partial theory" advocates raised a number of penetrating complaints against inerrancy, inciting careful reflection and thoughtful rebuttal on the part of those endorsing the high view. Conservatives tried to harmonize alleged discrepancies and inconsistencies in their doctrine, arguing that Scripture and the secular sciences would always agree if properly interpreted.

Chapter three examines the growing controversy over inerrancy throughout the second half of the nineteenth-century—from around 1860–1900—the pre-dawn of fundamentalism. Increasingly, nervous fidgeting became a common posture among biblical scholars of this time period, as the encroachments of geology, Darwinism, the rise of liberal theology, and the challenges of text critical theories, continued challenging biblical authority and integrity.

Some scholars, hoping to preserve the credibility of revealed religion and the Christian faith, bolted from the traditional posture, introducing and endorsing theories of inspiration which were less rigid. By focusing on the spiritual message of the Bible rather than its historical or scientific teachings, these scholars hoped to insulate the "main" message of Scripture from ridicule.

Debates centering on the acceptability of belief in an errorless Bible became increasingly common and heated. In the face of growing secular opposition, endorsing biblical inerrancy exposed the Christian faith to unnecessary derision, some scholars urged. Partial theory advocates believed that errors of fact existed in Scripture but were inconsequential, incapable of tarnishing the vibrant spiritual message of the Bible. However, proponents of the high view of inspiration disagreed, remaining dedicated to an inerrant biblical record.

Chapter four takes a closer look at one of the principal debates that occurred in the second half of the nineteenth-century. In the late nineteenth-century one of the truly sensational heresy trials in America was convened—the case of Professor Charles A. Briggs of Union Seminary. The Briggs case is fascinating and pivotal, explaining as it does the roots of the modern criticism condemning inerrancy.

The concluding chapter reflects over the modern debate using the nineteenth-century historical analysis as a backdrop. The assertion that inerrancy is a novelty is exposed as incorrect. Rather than innovators, fundamentalists are cast as the standard-bearers of the ascendant theory of biblical authority commonly endorsed among many of the leading Protestant elite in nineteenth-century America.

A historiographical postlude appears in the appendix that examines the article written by A. A. Hodge and Warfield in which they supposedly invented inerrancy. Since the critical theorists accuse them of innovative and evasive measures, it seems appropriate to consider their censure specifically and directly. A bibliography is offered next, providing a helpful roadmap for those interested in pursuing their own investigative research more fully.

1

The Doctrine of Inspiration

The Key to Biblical Authority

THROUGHOUT the history of Christianity the doctrine of biblical inspiration has been inextricably connected to, and in fact determined, the nature and extent of biblical authority—they have been two sides of the same coin. If God composed the Scripture, using human writers as his amanuensis, it logically followed that everything contained therein, whether pertaining to matters of faith or fact, must be without error— how could deity make a mistake? If, on the other hand, only some parts of Scripture possessed such divine markings or if only the thoughts and not the words came forth from God, one might argue—as some did—that the Bible's authority was limited, consisting only of those admonitions, precepts, or doctrines judged evident of divine composition.

Many nineteenth-century theological elite among the Presbyterians, Congregationalists, Methodists, and Baptists, maintained that the Bible, in its original autographs, in every part, including matters of history and science, was divinely composed and protected from all error, right down to the very words. Proponents asserted that Scripture wielded complete divine authority, representing the actual voice of God. This authority included issues of faith and religious practice to be sure, but it went far further than this. Adherents contended that Scripture spoke with authority on matters pertaining to history, geography, science, and anything else addressed by the divine author. Human responsibility consisted in determining, to the highest degree possible, the genuine reading of the original autographs, and humbly complying with its instructions, exhortations, precepts, and doctrines. Theological elite on all sides of the debate considered this the "high" or "strict" view of inspiration.

The "Partial theory" of inspiration, represented largely by the Unitarians, liberal Congregationalists, and other free thinkers, tended to stress human judgment as the arbiter over the sacred text in determining which portions of the Bible expressed sentiments commensurate with the divine mind and which did not.[1] The interpreter only embraced those principles and concepts that they deemed evident of holy origin, discarding those notions which appeared contrary to reason. Thus human reason became the adjudicator for determining whether any given biblical passage expressed divine or profane instruction.

Throughout the nineteenth-century, Protestant religious leaders engaged in a spirited and sometimes combative debate regarding the extent and nature of divine inspiration of the Bible. It is no hyperbole to suggest that many of the leading minds of Protestantism considered not only the welfare of the church but its very existence to hinge rather precariously on this issue. This angst is clear from the statements made by one Methodist scholar writing in 1819. He noted, "Nothing could be more evident than that a firm belief in their [the Scriptures] Inspiration is of the highest moment, not only to the edification and peace of the church, but in a great measure to its existence; for if this be given up, the authority of the revelation is enervated, and its use destroyed."[2] And a decade later, one of the leading voices at Andover seminary prophesied somewhat ominously, ". . . if I mistake not the signs of the times, this subject [biblical inspiration and inerrancy] is likely, before long, to form the dividing line between those who adhere to the evangelical doctrines of our forefathers, and those who renounce them."[3]

The Majority View: Inerrancy of the Autographs

A careful perusal of the antebellum scholarly literature indicates that inerrancy pervaded the highest levels of Protestantism from the very beginning of the century. Many theologians insisted that the Bible, in all its parts, extending to the very words, and including matters of history and science as well as faith and practice, was necessarily perfect and without mistake.[4]

1. William Ellery Channing stands out as one of the foremost proponents of this view of Scripture in the early nineteenth-century. Channing argued that reason reigned as judge over the sacred text, writing, "If, after a deliberate and impartial use of our best faculties, a professed revelation seems to us plainly to disagree with itself or to clash with great principles which we cannot question, we ought not to hesitate to withhold from it our belief. I am surer that my rational nature is from God than that any book is an expression of his will." Lyttle, *Liberal Gospel*, 129.

2. "On the Divine Authority of the Sacred Scriptures," 320–24.

3. Woods, *Lectures on the Inspiration of the Scriptures*, vii.

4. Verbal inspiration and the errorless quality of the Bible are recurrent themes in the

The statement made by one scholar writing in the *Theological and Literary Journal* is indicative of those on verbal inspiration found elsewhere, "To affirm, therefore, that the inspiration of the sacred writers was a mere inspiration of thoughts unassociated with language, is to affirm an impossibility . . . and is in effect to deny that they have any inspiration."[5] These biblical scholars believed that the divine nature of Scripture extended to the words of the text.

This verbally errorless quality, they quickly pointed out, applied only to the original autographs as they came from the hand of the sacred penmen. They did not consider copyists inspired, nor did these scholars expect the transcripts to be flawless replications of the autographs.[6] Indeed, from the very beginning of the nineteenth-century scholars recognized the presence of textual variants within the extant copies, often appealing to this fact as a rebuttal to alleged contradictions in the text. As early as 1800, the Swedish theologian John Dick articulated this very idea writing:

> While we admire the care of Divine Providence in the preservation of the scriptures, we do not affirm that all the transcribers of them were miraculously guarded against all error. Various motives . . . contributed to render them scrupulously careful; but that they were under no infallible guidance, is evident from the different readings, which are discovered by a collation of manuscripts, and the mistakes in matters of greater or less importance, observable

---

scholarly theological literature of the journal archives. Among others see: Woods, *Lectures*, 88, 92; Alexander, "Review of Woods on Inspiration," 18; Lee, *Inspiration of Holy Scripture*, 337; Pond, "Lee on Inspiration," 33, 53; Torrey and Burlington, "Essay on Inspiration," 334; "Geographical Accuracy of the Bible," 451–52, and 463; Robinson ed. "Rawlinson's Historical Evidences," 505, 510–11; Hodge, "Inspiration of Holy Scripture," 674–75; Lord ed. "Inspiration of the Scriptures, its Nature and Extent," 25.

5. Lord ed. "Inspiration of the Scriptures, its Nature and Extent," 25. Charles Hodge affirmed precisely the same doctrine in the same year stating, "The guidance of the sacred writers extended to the words no less than to thoughts of the sacred writers . . . the guidance of the Spirit extended to the words employed . . . To deny, in such cases, the control of the Spirit over the words of the sacred writers, is to deny inspiration altogether . . . The view, therefore, everywhere presented in the New Testament of the inspiration of the ancient prophets, supposes them to be under the guidance of the Holy Spirit in the selection of the words they employ . . . But how anyone can hold that the sacred writers were inspired as to their thoughts, but not as to their language, is to us perfectly incomprehensible." Hodge, "Inspiration of Holy Scripture," 675–77. Hodge iterated some years later, "The thoughts are in the words, the two are inseparable." Hodge, *Systematic Theology*, 1:164.

6. Since some modern scholars view the inerrancy of the autograph doctrine with great suspicion, it seems worthwhile to briefly chronicle its presence within several mainline denominations. Indeed, antebellum biblical scholars appealed to the perfection of the original manuscripts with great frequency as shall be demonstrated presently.

in them all. A contradiction, which could not be imputed to the
blunder of a transcriber, but was fairly chargeable on the sacred
writers themselves, would completely disprove their inspiration.[7]

Dick explicitly stated that his confidence in the doctrine of inspiration reposed upon absolute perfection in the originals, noting that the
presence of a genuine contradiction between the sacred penmen would
abnegate their divinely inspired status. The Holy Spirit, the clandestine
composer of Scripture, could never err.

In a later work on theology, published after his death, Dick once
again discussed the importance of ascertaining the reading of the original
autographs stating:

> We do not possess the original copies of the sacred writings. The
> autographs of the apostles and prophets have long since disappeared
> . . . It may be presumed, that the persons employed in transcribing
> the sacred writings would be at great pains to make the copies accu-
> rate . . . Yet, without a miracle, every transcript could not have been
> a faultless representation of the original; and that no supernatural
> influence was exerted upon their minds, may be very confidently
> inferred from the different readings which appear upon a collation
> of manuscripts. It is certain that they cannot all be right, and it is
> probable that not one of them is perfectly correct . . . No single
> manuscript can be supposed to exhibit the original text, without
> the slightest variation; it is to be presumed, that in all manuscripts,
> errors more or fewer in number are to be found.[8]

By acknowledging this, Dick expressed the conventional wisdom of the
day that no text was absolutely perfect; each needed to be examined against
the available textual evidence. Lower textual critics, who had conducted
this sort of exacting manuscript work for centuries, labored to determine
the original readings on the assumption that they represented the divine
voice precisely.

7. Dick, *Essay on the Inspiration of the Holy Scriptures*, 186–87.

8 Widely heralded as a classic on both sides of the Atlantic, Dick's *Essay* went through
multiple publications, exerting sustained and substantial influence. The brief chronology
of its widespread appearance is as follows: published in Edinburgh in 1800 by Ogle and
Aikman, published in Boston by Lincoln and Edmans in 1811, published in Glasgow in
1813, published again in Philadelphia in 1818, published by the Society for the Diffusion
of Christianity in New York in 1835, published again in Glasgow in 1840, and finally
published again in Boston in 1871. Impressively, the work remained vital and in broad currency, receiving great respect from students of biblical authority for nearly three-quarters of
a century. *The National Union Catalog*, 142:545.
Dick, *Lectures on Theology*, 1:122–24.

As early as 1825, this same sort of concession appeared in *The Biblical Repertory*, a journal edited by Charles Hodge. In the first edition of the journal C. Beck wrote,

> The scrupulous care taken of the Sacred Writings, and the custom of using them constantly in the church, is sufficient to convince us that they have been preserved from all serious alterations, yet they could not be entirely defended from the fate of all other ancient writings. The autographs appear to have perished early, and the copies which were taken, became more or less subject to those errors, which arise from the mistakes of transcribers, the false corrections of commentators and critics, from marginal notes, and from other sources.[9]

Theologians had grown accustomed to the sort of vexing problems associated with transcriber errors, making the quest for the original readings vitally important.

Indeed, the autograph doctrine played a consistently crucial role in biblical study throughout the first half of the century. Both Leonard Woods and Robert Haldane, writing in 1829 and 1830 respectively, discuss their importance. Woods, a professor of theology for nearly four decades at Andover Seminary, reasoned, "Instances of incorrectness in the present copies of the Scriptures cannot be objected to the inspiration of the writers. How can the fact, that God has not infallibly guided all who transcribe his word, prove that he did not infallibly guide those who originally wrote it?"[10] His conviction regarding the significance of the original autographs only intensified, ossifying over the next decade and a half. Writing in 1844 Woods stated,

> The objection to the plenary inspiration of the Scriptures, from the inaccuracy of the translations, and the various readings of the ancient manuscripts, is totally irrelevant. For what we assert is, the inspiration of the original Scriptures, not of the translations, or the ancient copies. The fact that the Scriptures were divinely inspired, cannot be expunged or altered by any subsequent event . . . The integrity of the copies has nothing to do with the inspiration of the original. It is, however, well known that the variations are hardly worth mentioning.[11]

9. Beck, "Monogrammata Hermeneutices," 27.

10. Woods, *Lectures on Inspiration*, 34–35.

11. Woods, "Inspiration of the Scriptures," 16.

Robert Haldane, writing in 1830 noted, "Inspiration belongs to the original writings. No one contends for any degree of inspiration in the transcribers in different ages."[12] Having noted this, Haldane went on to insist that the existing copies possessed an exceedingly high degree of accuracy, assured both by the providence of God and the large number of extant manuscripts which could be compared one against the other.[13]

The testimony of Enoch Pond, Congregational clergyman and professor at Bangor Theological Seminary, further demonstrates the broad acceptance of the doctrine of the inerrancy of the original autographs. While offering a rave review of the book by William Lee supporting verbal plenary inspiration and inerrancy, Pond noted,

> It should be understood, however, that when speaking of the inspiration of the sacred writings, we refer only to the original copies. We refer to them as they were when they came from the hands of the inspired penmen. We do not believe in the inspiration of transcribers, or translators, or interpreters.[14]

Interestingly, in this review, written in 1858, Pond posed a question from an imaginary critic who might censure the original autograph doctrine based on the fact that no original documents existed. Pond responded to his phantom interloper by arguing that an errorless original was vital:

> But we do think it of great importance to have had an *inspired and infallible original.* From such an original, all the existing copies and versions came; and, though we have not the autographs with which to compare them, still we can compare them with one another; we can judge of differences, where they exist; we can judge wherein they differ, if at all, from the inspired copies; and can thus approximate, at least to the true standard.[15]

Baptist scholars also endorsed inerrancy. In January 1855 an article published in the *Freewill Baptist Quarterly* argued that verbal inspiration and inerrancy ". . . relates only to the original production of the books of Scripture, and denotes that divine superintendence of their production, which secured them from error."[16] While the author considered the existing manuscripts highly reliable reproductions, he did "not claim for any

---

12. Haldane, *Genuineness and Authenticity of the Holy Scriptures*, 91.

13. Ibid.

14. Pond, "Lee on Inspiration," 34.

15. Ibid., 47–48.

16. Woods, "Inspiration of the Scriptures," 34.

translation the inspiration that belongs to the original."[17] Further express-ing his commitment to inerrancy he wrote,

> The remaining view, and which is now generally adopted by the church, is, that the whole of the Bible is inspired—that God so superintended its original publication, both in the matter and the manner of its contents, as to secure it from error; as much as though every word of it had been written by his own finger.[18]

This position remained consistent across time among Baptist scholars. Lemuel Moss, writing in the *Baptist Quarterly* over a decade later reinforced the Baptist commitment to the original autograph theory, writing,

> Of course inspiration can be predicated only of the original Scriptures, because they only are the writings of inspired men. There is no evidence that these books have been miraculously preserved from errors of transmission. . . . Nor can translators and interpret-ers, or their work, claim exemption from human infirmity.[19]

The Baptist theologian, Alvah Hovey, affirmed the same doctrine a decade later, endorsing the inerrancy of the sacred writings and "their marvel-ous accuracy of statement in matters which can be tested." Hovey noted that this errorless character applied only "as they came from the hands of inspired men, and not as we have them now in the best editions of the New Testament."[20]

Just as with Enoch Pond, Hovey anticipated possible objections to the doctrine of inerrancy based upon the missing manuscripts—is it not absurd one might argue to endorse an original autograph theory since no autographs were extant? What good are the copies? Hovey raised a possible objection to the autograph theory, writing, "The Bible, it is said cannot be the infallible word of God:—*Because infallibility in the original Scriptures requires for its complement infallibility in all copies, translations, and, some would say, interpretations of them.*"[21] Hovey disagreed, defending the autograph doctrine, noting:

> But this, again, is a mistake; for the errors from transcription, translations, &c., are such as can be detected, or at least elimi-

---

17. Ibid., 43.
18. Ibid., 34
19. Moss, "Dr. Curtis on Inspiration," 106.
20. Hovey, *Manual of Systematic Theology*, 79–80.
21. Ibid., 83–84.

nated, and reduced to a minimum; while errors in the original revelation could not be measured.[22]

Presbyterian scholars had no inclination to wait for young Hodge and Warfield before endorsing the inerrancy of the original autographs. Writing in the *Southern Presbyterian Review* in 1851, One Presbyterian divine argued in favor of the plenary inspiration of the Bible, noting an important qualification to his position:

> When we say that the Scriptures are divinely inspired throughout, we do not speak of translations or copies, but of the original writings. For the Almighty to direct the pens of the sacred writers is one thing, and it is quite another for him to guide, infallibly, the pens of all in every age who may copy or translate or quote the Bible.[23]

22. Ibid., 84.

23. "Plenary Inspiration of the Scriptures," 469. Of course, this is only the tip of the theological iceberg concerning the Presbyterians. As we shall see shortly, Archibald Alexander and Charles Hodge, the great Princeton luminaries, both explicitly endorsed the inerrancy of the original manuscripts. Another highly regarded Presbyterian divine delivered an important sermon in 1855 that presents more thorny obstacles to the critical theory which insists that inerrancy was a late-nineteenth-century fabrication. The Presbyterian Synod of New York and New Jersey requested Henry B. Smith, Professor at Union Theological Seminary, to present a sermon to them on the inspiration of Scripture. Smith cordially obliged and prepared a presentation for this august body entitled, "The Inspiration of the Holy Scriptures." Even then, a controversy over this matter was evidently brewing, one to which Smith referred directly in the introduction of his message. Among other things, in his address Smith spoke specifically to the three principal complaints registered by Sandeen against A. A. Hodge and B. B. Warfield as innovative. Sandeen urges that verbal inspiration, the inspiration of the original manuscripts, and the belief that Scripture taught its own inspired status combined to serve as a calculated theological dodge intended to insulate Scripture from critical assaults. However, Smith considered each one of these tenets as entirely orthodox and essential to a correct doctrine of inspiration. Concerning the autographs, Smith repeatedly argued that inspiration extended only to the "original Scriptures," saying this on three occasions in his discourse. The modern interpreter is impressed by the fact that Smith offered no explanation as to what he intended by using this term, indicating that no elaboration was necessary. It appears to be a rudimentary principle readily accessed by the elite. Smith stated ". . . the original canonical Scriptures . . . are given by a Divine Inspiration . . . and are the Word of God, and as such, an infallible and final authority." Smith further stated that inspiration included the precise words of the original text saying, "It comprises both the matter and form of the Bible; the matter in the form in which it is conveyed and set forth. It extends even to the language . . . . They spake as they were moved by the Holy Ghost." Furthermore, Smith appealed to at least two dozen biblical passages that he insisted endorsed the divine inspiration of Scripture. He believed that the Bible taught its own divinely inspired status, making it the flawless word of God. Regarding inspiration, Smith urged "Its object is the communication of truth in an infallible manner, so that, when rightly interpreted, no error is conveyed." Smith, "Inspiration of the Holy Scriptures," 1855.

Neither were Methodists lagging behind in a commitment to inerrancy, endorsing it in a number of scholarly publications. Richard Watson applied the perfection of the text strictly to the original copies, stating that the "manuscripts now extant are, confessedly, liable to errors and mistakes from the carelessness, negligence or inaccuracy of copyists."[24] Emphasizing the importance of lower text criticism, Watson continued, "but they are not all uniformly incorrect throughout, nor in the same words or passages; but what is incorrect in one place is correct in another."[25] Determining the precise readings of the original documents represented a lofty scholarly endeavor, because once attained, the reader possessed the words of God.

In explaining the importance of lower biblical criticism, D. A. Whedon discussed its exacting nature. Clarifying the original text of the autographs represented a crucial enterprise because those words possessed an inspired status. Whedon stated:

> Biblical criticism aims at ascertaining the precise words of Holy Scripture as they stood in the original autographs of the sacred writers. Those words were true, authoritative, inspired. Were those autographs producible, they would at once settle the whole question of the text to which the lives of some of the noblest scholars of the last three centuries have been given; but they long since perished . . . The labor is to ascertain the exact language, even to the insertion of an article, the orthography of a word, the inflection of a noun, the mood and tense of a verb, so that we shall have "the words which the Holy Ghost teacheth."[26]

Whedon praised efforts to recapture the original readings—down to the tiniest detail.

Thus, it is clear that the original autograph doctrine was a basic tenet in the writings of the Presbyterians, Congregationalists, Baptists, and Methodists. Many seminaries like Bangor and most especially Andover demonstrated as sturdy a commitment to the idea as did Princeton. It pervaded the highest levels of Protestantism from the very beginning of the nineteenth-century.

Furthermore, the primary evidence to which these scholars appealed in support of this doctrine came from the Bible itself. So convinced were they that Scripture taught its own divine origin that they stood resolute against all encroachments by science, believing that the author of nature

---

24. Watson, *Theological Institutes*, 1:149.

25. Ibid.

26. Whedon, "Greek Text of the New Testament," 325.

could in no way contradict the author of Scripture, being one and the same.[27] Leonard Woods noted in this regard,

> The argument upon which the doctrine of inspiration should be made chiefly to rest, is the testimony of the sacred writers themselves. . . . The inspiration of the sacred writers is a fact. For information respecting this fact, and respecting its extent, its degree, and its results we are dependent mainly on them.[28]

Neither were these scholars atypical in their outlook on Scripture. It appears certain that the high view represented both the majority opinion and the traditional view for a number of reasons. First, proponents assumed that they represented the traditional, dominant viewpoint. Leonard Woods, among others, considered the high view of inspiration both the orthodox and the prevailing theory at the time.[29] Of course, this could simply mean that they were aggressive or arrogant; but, secondly, opponents readily ceded the historical high ground to the inerrant opinion.[30]

For instance, as early as 1830 one Unitarian scholar, arguing in favor of the partial theory, admitted that the high view of inspiration represented the "prevailing theological assumptions in regard to our sacred books," and that it was "the common theory of inspiration."[31] Third, since much of the antebellum criticism questioning the authority and integrity of Scripture

27. Biblical scholars who endorsed inerrancy constantly sought to substantiate their position by appealing to Scripture. They maintained their commitment to inerrancy, not because of a rationalistic philosophy, but because of their careful exegetical analysis of the text of the Bible. This is clearly evident throughout the literature and is illustrated in William Lee's treatise on inspiration in which he devoted 40 pages to the Scriptural evidences for the high view of inspiration.

28. Woods, *Lectures*, 18.

29. Ibid., vii.

30. Even George Ladd, an outspoken late nineteenth-century critic of the inerrancy of the autograph position, conceded that it was in fact the ascendant view "without dispute in Protestant theology from the close of the sixteenth-century to the middle of the eighteenth-century. . . ." While the theory fell from favor in Europe under the influence of German higher criticism and Romantic philosophy; the "old orthodoxy" continued to dominate in America, evidenced by Ladd's continuing efforts to overtake it in the United States as late as 1883. Ladd, *Doctrine of Sacred Scripture*, 452. Furthermore, an even earlier critic of inerrancy, Samuel Taylor Coleridge, lamented the fact that it represented the dominant theory of biblical authority in the first half of the nineteenth-century, writing, "notwithstanding the repugnancy of the doctrine, in its unqualified sense, to Scripture, Reason, and Common Sense . . . I must still avow my belief that . . . it *is* the Doctrine which the generality of our popular divines receive as orthodox . . ." Coleridge, *Confessions of an Inquiring Spirit*, 42.

31. "Review of Leonard Woods *Lectures on the Inspiration of the Scriptures,*" 362–65.

was based on advances made by geology, the critical theory necessarily represented a new viewpoint, since geology itself was a new science.

Evidence of a growing debate over biblical authority appears not only in the journal archive, but in a number of books as well. Volumes appeared in the decades of the twenties, thirties, forties, and fifties, endorsing and defending inerrancy, suggesting increasing concern among high view advocates. Leonard Woods, writing in the 1820s, and William Lee, who produced a major work on inspiration in the 1850s, are representative of the kind of apologetic frequently made in favor of the high view position.

Woods served as the chair of Christian Theology at Andover Theological Seminary for thirty-eight years, teaching over fifteen-hundred ministerial students during his tenure.[32] Andover, begun in 1808, functioned as one of the key training centers for Congregational and Presbyterian ministers. Woods produced a concise book in 1829 based on a lecture series he had delivered at Andover during the preceding years. Viewing himself as part of a continuing legacy of theologians who supported the high view of inspiration, Woods answered common objections to this view and marshaled many arguments in its favor throughout the book.

He constructed the case for verbal plenary inspiration and inerrancy principally from the Scriptures themselves, arguing for the divine authorship, first, of the Old Testament, by appealing to New Testament evidence. Conservatives consistently summoned two key passages of the New Testament as witnesses for the divine nature of Scripture: 2 Pet 1:21 and 2 Tim 3:16. Almost every advocate of the high view of inspiration made reference to these texts as offering conclusive evidence in their favor. Woods was no different. Arguing from both a grammatical and contextual basis, Woods favored the predicate use for the adjective "God-breathed" found in 2 Tim 3:16, rendering the meaning of the phrase as "all Scripture *is* God-breathed."[33]

---

32. Walker, *Ten New England Leaders*, 386. Walker provides a helpful biographical treatment of Woods in this work on pages 365–401. The biographer quotes from Woods' "Dedicatory Address" delivered to his students. Woods' commitment to Scriptural authority is evident in this professorial advice offered to his pupils, "I entreat you to keep at the greatest distance from all unscriptural speculations, and to repose unlimited confidence in the word of God . . . There is, in my view, no ground of safety but a serious, unquestioning belief, resulting from thorough examination and Christian experience, that all Scripture is divinely inspired—that the whole Bible was written under the special guidance of the Holy Spirit, and is consequently clothed with divine authority, and is infallible in all its teachings. Hold fast to this principle, and you are safe." Walker, *Leaders*, 392. Woods' position on the Bible did not waver during his thirty eight year tenure at Andover.

33. In the King James translation of the Bible 2 Pet 1:21 reads, "For the prophecy came

This passage offered high view advocates a full endorsement for the divine nature of whatever constituted "Scripture." As such, divine authorship clearly pertained to every part of the Old Testament, resulting in a perfect record in matters pertaining to either faith or facts. Woods believed in the verbal inspiration of the text, noting,

> But as the writers of Scripture nowhere limit the divine influence which they enjoyed to the conception of their own minds; neither would I do it. And as there are some texts, which, according to any fair interpretation, clearly imply that the divine guidance . . . had, in an important sense, a respect to their language; how can I entertain any further doubt?[34]

Woods also argued that the way in which Christ and the apostles regarded the Old Testament endorsed its inspired, inerrant status. Jesus, Woods contended, fully subscribed to the inerrancy of the Jewish Scriptures, bestowing upon them full divine sanction. The apostles constantly appealed to them assuming that they possessed inspired authority. Nowhere do the apostles or Christ ever give the slightest indication that these books were anything other than perfectly accurate in every detail, Woods argued.[35] Nor did Christ or his colleagues ever offer the slightest hint or suggestion that some parts of the Old Covenant had less authority than other parts or were inspired in differing degrees.

Since the New Testament eclipsed the glory of the Old, the record constituting it must be of equal authority and perfection, Woods reasoned. Offering further evidence for this, Woods noted that the apostles received special promises from Christ for infallible guidance in their ministry, receiving their commission by him as teachers of the Christian religion. Doubters needed only to look to the miracles performed by their hands to find confirmation of their authority. Furthermore, the apostles, Woods noted, believed themselves to be agents of God operating as they wrote under his divinely infallible instructions, citing many biblical passages in support of his claim. According to Woods, the Bible was a divine product

---

not in old time by the will of man: but holy men of God spake as they were moved by the Holy Ghost." In the same translation 2 Tim 3:16 states, "All Scripture is given by inspiration of God (God-breathed) and is profitable for doctrine, for reproof, for correction, and for instruction in righteousness." Significant debates centered on whether the Greek adjective rendered "inspired" or "God-breathed" in 2 Tim 3 functioned attributively or in the predicate sense. Though sometimes translated "inspired" the literal meaning of the term is "God-breathed."

34. Woods, *Lectures*, 92.

35. Ibid., 66.

completely exempt from any taint of error, though this incorruptible status applied solely to the original manuscripts as they came from the hands of the sacred writers. In summarizing another key section Woods succinctly defined the high view of inspiration, stating,

> this one point I think is specially important to maintain; namely, *that the sacred writers had such direction of the Holy Spirit, that they were secured against all liability to error, and enabled to write just what God pleased; so that what they wrote is, in truth, the word of God, and can never be subject to any charge of mistake either as to matter or form.*[36]

William Lee, writing in the 1850s, produced one of the most comprehensive books in support of the inerrant view of the Scriptures. Though Lee taught at Trinity College Dublin, his book had a substantial influence in America as evidenced both by its many printings and its widespread review by American scholars.[37] Lee stoutly argued, as those before him had, that the Bible, in all its parts, whether pertaining to history or science, right down to the exact words and phrases, was without error because God wrote it. As the product of divine composition, if properly understood, it would always prove true and accurate.[38]

Furthermore, Lee contended that the Bible had nothing to fear from the advances of science, because God who created both the Bible and the natural world could never truly conflict.[39] The Bible's authority extended to both faith and fact, for Lee viewed them as very much the same thing. He noted, "We must ever regard as both unfounded and superficial that view of inspiration which distinguishes, in the sacred narrative, between matters of fact and matters of doctrine. In the Christian faith matters of fact exhibit and convey doctrines; while the doctrines are presented to us as matters of fact."[40]

---

36. Ibid., 96.

37. Lee's book was eagerly received and voraciously consumed in America. This fact is evidenced by its numerous publications and printings here. His book, *The Inspiration of the Holy Scriptures*, was published in America by Robert Carter and Brothers in 1857, 1858, 1860, 1866, and 1868. Not only did Americans hail its publication, so too did readers in Great Britain as made clear by its numerous publications there as well. It went through several editions in London, being published in 1854, 1864, and 1865. *National Union Catalog*, 323:146–47. Moreover, both conservative and liberal American scholars gave Lee's work a thorough review in the literature.

38. Lee, *Inspiration of Holy Scripture*, 342.

39. Ibid., 373–74.

40. Ibid., 334–35.

Not only did Lee argue for the flawless reliability of all the facts of Scripture, but he also supported the full inspiration of every word and phrase of the Bible, stating, "even the form and language in which its truths are expressed bear the impress of its divine origin . . . from the nature of the reasoning by our Lord and his Apostles in which it is invariably assumed that the *words* of Scripture are no less Divine than the doctrines which they convey."[41] He went on to buttress his point by demonstrating occasions in which the argument of the biblical writer hinged upon a single word, or a Greek verb tense, or the use of a singular rather than a plural noun. All these fine subtleties, Lee argued, substantiated an inspiration theory which included the words as well as the ideas.

That Lee based his outlook on the Scriptures can hardly be contested, since he devoted over forty pages to the biblical evidences for verbal plenary inspiration. He prefaced this portion of his work by stating, "The value of the inspired writers' own statements is naturally of the highest order. Those statements fully confirm the hereditary doctrine of the Church upon the subject of Inspiration."[42] Both Lee and Woods stand as significant proponents of the high view of inspiration, in part, because Princeton theologians applauded their scholarly contributions to the literature.

Archibald Alexander, the first professor at Princeton Seminary, reviewed the book by Leonard Woods on inspiration soon after it came out. Alexander gave a strong endorsement to the ideas expressed by Woods on inspiration, agreeing with him on every significant issue, though he expressed less appreciation for the literary style of the Andover professor. Alexander wrote,

---

41. Ibid., 337.

42. Ibid., 237–38. A significant footnote appears in this section of Lee's book. On 239 Lee records in a note, "I cannot avoid alluding to the manner in which Perrone copies, as one may say, the words of the most extreme Rationalists, in his desire to prove that the authority of the Church is the *sole* ground for our belief in the inspiration of Scripture." The accusation that rationalist philosophy precipitated the commitment to the doctrine of inerrancy of the original autographs seems to be a recurrent one. Recently, James Barr in his criticism of fundamentalism echoes the very same charge made by Perrone against the inerrantists of his day, writing, "Nowhere is the rationalism of fundamentalist argument more clear than in the doctrine of the inspiration and infallibility of the Bible itself. Though inspiration is mentioned in the Bible, nowhere does the Bible suggest that inspiration includes the package of implications taken as authoritative by fundamentalists; it nowhere says that this implies historical accuracy, it nowhere says anything about the original autographs, indeed it no where says that Jesus commanded or authorized the writing of the New Testament at all. The fundamentalist construction is not derived from what Scripture actually says but is derived *rationally*." Barr, *Scope and Authority of the Bible*, 70.

Dr. Woods's definition of inspiration is 'a supernatural guidance or assistance afforded to the sacred writers, that divine guidance or assistance having been such as to entirely guard them against error . . .' Although we do not admire the way in which the thing is expressed, yet we concur with Dr. Woods entirely in his views of the plenary nature of that inspiration by which the Scripture was written. His views also, on the subject of the manner in which inspiration must affect language, as well as the ideas of the books of Scripture, are, in our opinion just.[43]

In his classic book, *Evidences of Christianity* published in 1837, Alexander offered his own definition of inspiration in which he thoroughly endorsed inerrancy. He stated,

The true definition of inspiration, then, is SUCH A DIVINE INFLUENCE UPON THE MINDS OF THE SACRED WRITERS AS RENDERED THEM EXEMPT FROM ERROR, BOTH IN REGARD TO THE IDEAS AND WORDS. This is properly called PLENARY inspiration. Nothing can be conceived more satisfactory. Certainty, infallible certainty, is the most that can be desired in any narrative; and if we have this in the sacred Scriptures, there is nothing more to be wished in regard to this matter.[44]

Employing capital letters, Alexander seemed intent upon making his position unmistakably clear. A number of important themes emerge from this definition: (1) all the writers of Scripture worked under a divine influence; (2) this divine influence rendered them incapable of error; (3) this exemption from mistakes applied to both the ideas and the words of the text; and thus (4) Alexander considered the biblical product infallible, without defect in any way, completely certain in every respect. Woods and Alexander united on the matter of biblical authority and inspiration.

In 1857, a second Princeton theologian, Charles Hodge, assessed the work on inspiration by William Lee. The admiration with which Hodge esteemed the work of Lee could scarcely have been greater. In offering a complete endorsement of Lee's book, Hodge revealed his own commitment to the infallibility of the Bible. Affirming his belief in verbal inspiration, Charles Hodge wrote:

The guidance of the Spirit extended to the words no less than to the thoughts of the sacred writers . . . the guidance of the Spirit

43. Alexander, "Review of Woods on Inspiration," 18.
44. Alexander, *Evidences of Christianity*, 230.

extended to the words employed . . . To deny, in such cases, the control of the Spirit over the words of the sacred writers, is to deny inspiration altogether . . . The view, therefore, everywhere present-ed in the New Testament of the inspiration of the ancient proph-ets, supposes them to be under the guidance of the Holy Spirit in the selection of the words they employ . . . But how anyone can hold that the sacred writers were inspired as to their thoughts, but not as to their language, is to us perfectly incomprehensible.[45]

Hodge thus explicitly argued in favor of verbal inspiration. Neither could Charles Hodge conceive of limiting inspiration to the thoughts alone. As he succinctly stated some years later, "The thoughts are in the words, the two are inseparable."[46]

Throughout his lengthy review, Hodge consistently supported Lee's notion of infallibility, arguing for the divine origin of all the Scriptures in all their parts, whether pertaining to history, science or matters of faith. He wrote, "In saying that the Bible is the word of God, we mean that he is the author; that he says whatever the Bible says; that everything which the Bible affirms to be true is true . . . because its declarations as to truth and duty, as to facts and principles, are the declarations of God."[47]

These Princeton reviews are illuminating for a number of reasons. First, the Princeton theologians were obviously not isolated loners or theological mavericks out of touch with mainstream Christian thought on biblical authority. Instead, the Princeton elite praised and endorsed the ideas of other important theologians on the matter of biblical authority. Second, both Alexander and Charles Hodge clearly endorsed the iner-rancy of the original autographs long before its alleged unveiling in the late nineteenth-century.

While many scholars endorsed inerrancy in the antebellum period, others did not. A number of alternate views regarding biblical authority existed. The following section outlines the two most prominent variations on the biblical doctrine of inspiration and the challenges they posed to the high view.

45. Hodge, "Inspiration ," 675–77.

46. Hodge, *Systematic Theology*, 1:164.

47. Hodge, "Inspiration," 663.

Alternative Views: The Partial Theory of Inspiration and the Degree Theory of Inspiration

The "partial theory" of inspiration, largely the product of the Unitarians and a growing number of Protestant liberals, was nuanced in two ways.[48] First, proponents argued that only certain passages of the Bible expressed the divine intellect, while other parts represented merely the fallible expressions and opinions of humans. Second, some others suggested that only the thoughts were inspired but not the language—the ideas were divine but not the words used to express them. Either way, the human interpreter functioned as the judge of Scripture; determining whether the text in question was sacred or secular.

A Unitarian review of the work by William Lee offers keen insight into the partial theory. After avowing a pious respect for the Bible and indeed a belief in its divine origin, the reviewer outlined many reasons for his position.[49] The reviewer raised a number of penetrating criticisms against the high view position. What of recent scientific discoveries? Where do they (the conservatives) stand, he asked, on the Copernican system of astronomy? Did they maintain with Moses "that the heavens are a solid concave, in which the sun, the planets and stars, like splendid balls of light, perform a daily revolution around the earth?"[50]

The partial theorists maintained that endorsing such misguided tenets discredited revealed religion far more radically than the belief in the existence of some contradictions and primitive errors in the text. They worried that pressing too hard on errorlessness would alienate the educated classes and lead to the eventual extinction of Christianity.[51] They looked upon

48. William Ellery Channing, a renowned leader of New England liberal thought, helped to form the American Unitarian Association in 1825. Though ill health prevented Channing from accepting the Presidency of the organization, he remained a central figure and powerful spokesman for the Unitarian viewpoint. Espousing what would become standard partial theory themes Channing noted, "We profess not to know a book which demands a more frequent exercise of reason than the Bible . . . its style nowhere affects the precision of science or the accuracy of definition. Its language is singularly glowing, bold, and figurative, demanding more frequent departures from the literal sense than that of our own age and country, and consequently demanding more continual exercise of judgment . . . we feel it our bounden duty to exercise our reason upon it perpetually, to compare, to infer, to look beyond the letter to the spirit, to seek in the nature of the subject and the aim of the writer his true meaning . . ." Lyttle, *Liberal Gospel*, 136–37.

49. "Review of *Lectures on the Inspiration of the Scriptures,*" 362–91.

50. Ibid., 366.

51. Channing expressed such worries and concerns even earlier, noting, "Men who, to support a creed, would shake our trust in the calm, deliberate, and distinct decisions of

passages of the Bible, such as the imprecations of David in the Psalms, in which David invoked curses upon his enemies, and shuddered to include them as representing the divine mind. Writing of David's diatribes the author stated,

> Indeed, there is no defense to be made of this passage. This could not have proceeded from the good and merciful spirit of God. It was the imperfection of David . . . It was the imperfection of a rude and barbarous age . . . Our reverence for the Psalmist is great; but we cannot be blind to the imperfection of such a passage as that which we have cited.[52]

Believing themselves to be both rational and reverent, the partial theorists considered their approach a far more enlightened one than that of their strict theory opponents. Moreover, they argued, the Bible contained many inconsequential matters that simply did not demand divine guidance to express. The passage in 2 Tim 4 in which Paul requested a cloak and some parchments from Timothy when the young man came to visit served as a favorite illustration of this assertion. Paul's admonition to Timothy to "take a little wine for thy stomachs sake" received equal ridicule as so trivial that to argue for its divine authorship actually impugned God's character as a composer of drivel, they urged. How could anyone, it was asserted, suppose that Paul was "specially directed" to say these things?

Furthermore, textual critics had long realized through careful exegetical analysis of the Bible that the human contributors retained a sense of their own unique personalities and styles as they composed the different books of Scripture. Comparing, for instance, Pauline literature with works written by Peter or John made these sorts of deductions clear. Some scholars argued that the presence of human personality indicated that the degree of divine control over the transmission process was less than complete.[53] How could the product of Scripture be at the same time both a human and divine composition?[54]

---

our rational and moral powers, endanger religion more than its open foes, and forge the deadliest weapon for the infidel." Lyttle, *Liberal Gospel*, 129.

52. "Review of *Lectures on the Inspiration of the Scriptures*," 367–68.

53. Ibid., 386.

54. Ibid. In jousting with Leonard Woods, this scholar chided, "Dr. Woods 'admits,' what it has been thought so great a fault in us to assert, that 'the language is completely human.' He admits, that 'in writing the Scriptures, the sacred penmen evidently made use of their own faculties;' that 'the language employed by the inspired writers exhibits no marks of a divine interference, but is perfectly conformed to the genius and tastes of the writers,' and that 'even the same doctrine is taught, and the same event described, in a different

Moreover, proponents of the partial theory tended to interpret some passages of Scripture differently than the conservatives. Nowhere did this disparity become more apparent than in the exegesis of 2 Tim 3:16. While scholars like Woods, Lee, Alexander and Hodge favored the predicate use of the adjective "God-breathed," resulting in the translation "all Scripture is God-breathed and is profitable. . . ." Partial theorists favored the attributive sense of the adjective, (in which the adjective attributed a quality to the noun "Scripture") rendering the passage to mean "all inspired Scripture is profitable." The attributive sense, rather than ascribing divine authority to all Scripture in all its parts, left the human interpreter to discern which parts of the Bible were inspired—and hence profitable—and which ones were not, a position most appealing in an age of reason.[55]

Another major criticism leveled against the inerrant school consisted of alleged contradictions and conflicts among and between the biblical writers. The fact that Mark and John differed as to the hour of Christ's passion or that the four gospel writers suggested different inscription readings above the cross, or that one gospel writer asserted the presence of but one angel at the tomb on Easter, while another said there were two, demonstrated, so critics alleged, that the Bible contained many contradictions. Doctrinal deviation between biblical writers also constituted a serious discrepancy, they asserted. The different means of redemption prescribed by Paul and James proved the classic case in point, in which the former endorsed salvation by faith in Christ alone while the latter supposedly included works in his economy of salvation.

Partial theorists also attacked the inerrant stance based on the vagaries of human language. How was it possible to achieve perfection in an instrument that by its very nature was unclear and incomplete? The reviewer noted,

---

manner by different writers.' And his constant answer is—very well; why not? Why should not the writers compose, each one, in his own style and manner? Why should they not, indeed, we say; but is this the proper answer to the objection? The objection is, that the style is natural, and therefore is not supernatural. The answer, admitting as it does the first quality, should show how the style can possess the other—or, in other words, how the same style could have been formed under influences at the same time natural and supernatural."

55. However, in his Greek grammar, A.T. Robertson notes that while it is remotely possible for the adjective in the present construction to function attributively, it is rare for it to do so. He notes "When the article is used before the adjective or participle, it is of course, attributive . . ." He goes on to note that while it is not impossible for the adjective to retain its attributive force without the article, in such cases as it does, the adjective normally appears before the noun. The adjective in 2 Tim 3:16 appears after the noun and without the article, making the predicate use highly likely. Robertson, *Grammar of the Greek New Testament,* 656.

> On this subject of the sacred style, we must beg our readers to have
> patience with us a moment longer . . . human language is, from
> its nature, essentially fallible; and it does appear to us, that if this
> point were fully considered, it would   settle the whole question
> about infallibility in the *words* of this communication. All human
> language, when referring to what is intellectual, to what is spiri-
> tual, is but an approximation to the truth . . . They are symbols,
> and they bear no relation to our intellectual conceptions, but what
> they bear by common agreement. Now this point we press. Was
> this agreement ever, in any age or country, perfect and invariable?
> . . . How then can the idea of absolute infallibility be attached to
> such an instrument of communication?[56]

Arguing that the general sense of a written message was all that could
ever be legitimately expected, the reviewer dismissed the notion of verbal
inerrancy as a guise developed by elites to retain power. Even textual critics
who explored the original languages with their grammars and dictionaries,
he noted, had to decide between as many as thirty lexical nuances for any
given word. As one keeps this in mind "all this solicitude about the perfect
verbal accuracy, the verbal authority of the Bible, in our apprehension,
is as useless as it is unphilosophical."[57] Therefore, only the ideas could be
inspired—the words were not.

The "Degree of Inspiration" theory, endorsed by some Methodists,
among others, argued that the various kinds of biblical literature; history, prophecy, poetry, didactic, narrative etc. required different levels or
degrees of divine intervention. One of the fathers of the degree theory,
Swedish theologian John Dick, argued that while the whole Bible was in
fact inspired, only some parts of it received direct revelation.

The degree of inspiration theory differed from the partial theory in
a number of important respects. First, while the partial theorists argued
that some portions of Scripture lacked an inspired status, degree advocates
did not make such an assertion. The Holy Spirit inspired the entire Bible
according to the degree theorists, although the manner of that inspiration
varied. Partial theory advocates admitted the presence of genuine errors and
contradictions in the Bible. The degree adherents admitted no such thing,
sounding very much like the plenarists in their commitments. Furthermore,
the partial theory made Scripture subservient to human reason—creating
a sort of biblical smorgasbord in which one could pick and choose one's
inspired version, a position the degree advocates clearly rejected.

56. "Review of *Lectures on the Inspiration of the Scriptures*," 389.
57. Ibid., 391.

Degree theorists suggested the presence of at least three levels of inspiration. The term "Superintendence" referred to the kind of divine oversight that occurred when the biblical writers recorded things to which they were already privy. When the writer possessed competency in the field to which he addressed his message, as in a historical account personally observed, the level of guidance needed was an inspiration of superintendence. At this level the Holy Spirit functioned as a supervisor, ensuring written accuracy but not necessarily directing the exact form of expression.

Superintendence thus represented the lowest level of divine agency and the most substantial degree of human activity. However, John Dick ascribed divine origin even to this level of inspiration, noting that even here, "the Holy Ghost led them on what to select . . . they [the biblical writers] rather resembled amanuenses, who commit to writing those things selected for them by their employer."[58] At this level the human contributors might express things crudely, but still without error.

"Elevation," a second and higher level of divine influence, furnished to the biblical writers a greater "vigor, conciseness and beauty of their productions, which might, without his aid, have been equally truthful, but less interesting and attractive."[59] This kind of aid produced literature that was at the same time completely truthful as well as beautiful—as one might find in the poetical literature or in the skillful use of imagery and metaphor.

"Suggestion," the third level, was direct revelation. The divine presence actually dictated the words to the sacred writer's mind, producing a text not only free from error but one entirely perfect in expression as well. It articulated the divine intellect verbatim. When was this sort of dictation model necessary? The Holy Spirit communicated at this level, they argued, when the biblical writer had no prior knowledge of the issue under consideration. Clearly this included all the prophetic literature in which God revealed truths previously unknown to human consciousness.

The degree theory permitted proponents to excuse the supposed crudities of the text without sacrificing its veracity. They nimbly dodged many of the criticisms lodged by the partial theorists against the conservatives. Under the inspiration of superintendence one expected the sacred penmen to write in their own unique fashion, secured as they were from mistakes but not from grammatical or syntactical incongruities.

The degree theory, though viewed as a serious departure from traditional orthodoxy by the verbal plenary advocates, actually aligned with

---

58. Dick, *Essay on the Inspiration of the Holy Scriptures,* 20.

59. Smith, "Inspiration of the Scriptures," 220.

them in its commitment to an errorless text, full inspiration of the biblical record, and even verbal inspiration. One degree theorist noted,

> Now a book, the contents of which are entirely true, may be said to be written by a *Full Inspiration*, though it contain many things, which the author might have known and recorded by the mere use of his natural faculties, if there be others which he did not know by these means, or could not, without miraculous assistance, have recollected so exactly; or on the whole, a freedom from all error would not in fact be found, unless God had superintended, and watched over his mind and pen.—Again, a book may be written by *Full Inspiration*, though the author being left to the choice of his own words, phrases and manner, there may be some imperfection in the style and method, provided the whole contents of it be *true*.[60]

That conservatives considered the degree theory heretical, a theory which affirmed the full inspiration and divine origin of the canonical record (though nuanced differently), underscores their tenacious commitment to inerrancy. By the close of the nineteenth-century doctrinal deviation of this sort would seem rather tame.

But how did high view advocates respond to the challenges raised against them by these competing theories—particularly the partial theory? How did they maintain their position and retain its integrity? Most especially, how did they answer the substantive charges of internal discrepancies within the text of Scripture itself and between the Bible and scientific advances, particularly in history, geography, and geology? The manner in which they answered their critics indicates their unrelenting commitment to the authority of the text of Scripture and their passionate belief that everything in the Bible, whether pertaining to matters of faith or fact was necessarily perfect—down to the very words.

---

60. "On the Divine Authority of the Sacred Scriptures," 382. (362—the pagination became confused)

2

Biblical Authority and the Sciences

High View Advocates Respond to Their Critics

I N many respects the degree of inspiration theory proved both less imposing and less complicated for the conservatives. Though it endorsed differing degrees of inspiration, it nonetheless considered the entire biblical product inspired—and thus error free. It never challenged the basic assumptions held dearest by the high view—namely, that the Bible was free from all errors and hence completely binding in all respects. If a proponent of the degree theory misjudged a passage of Scripture, attributing to it an inspiration of "elevation" rather than of "superintendence," not much practical harm ensued. Theoretically it mattered, but practically it remained benign. The passage, still representing the divine mind, demanded adherence and reverence—it retained authority.

Furthermore, virtually all the conservatives denounced the degree theory for the same reason—no biblical text discussed, suggested, or implied that degrees of inspiration existed. As one writer noted,

> The authors of the low and derogatory view of the word of God, which ascribes to it different degrees of inspiration, cannot plead a single passage that will afford them even the shadow of support. Their doctrine is but a theory—a theory in opposition to the most express assertions of Scripture, and not countenanced by the allegation of a single text.[1]

With this said, many conservatives felt satisfied. Thus, the degree theory posed a less serious threat to the inerrant position—both practically and exegetically. Since high view advocates felt justified to summarily dismiss it as without basis, it did not consume their attention in the same riveting manner as did the partial theory.

1. Haldane, *Genuineness and Authenticity of the Holy Scriptures*, vi.

The partial theory was much more challenging and threatening. After consigning a passage to nothing more than a mere human convention, the interpreter was free from all obligation to it—it wielded no authority. Furthermore, proponents would likely accept or discard different parts of Scripture, leading, conservatives feared, to chaos, anarchy, and schism.

The partial theory, conservatives concluded, eroded all confidence in an absolute, objective word from God. As high view proponents viewed things, the partial theory represented an all out assault on the authority and integrity of the Bible—and the future welfare of the Church. Clearly John Dick had this firmly in view when he warned,

> The denial of the plenary inspiration of the Scriptures tends to un-settle the foundations of our faith; involves us in doubt and perplex-ity; and leaves us no method of ascertaining how much we should believe, except an appeal to reason. But when reason is invested with the authority of a judge, not only is revelation dishonored, and its Author insulted, but the end for which it was given is com-pletely defeated. Instead of being admitted as the supreme standard of human opinions and practices in religion, it is degraded into a subordinate role, and possesses no more authority than the fallible and capricious wisdom of men will allow it to exercise.[2]

Employing the same defense mechanisms against the partial view, conservatives argued that it lacked biblical support. Human reason re-placed divine authorship as the ultimate source of authority, allowing different people to reject whatever proved unappealing to their spiritual palate. Enoch Pond noted in this regard,

> If it [the Bible] is not *all* inspired; then who shall tell us what par-ticular parts are inspired, and what not . . . One passage may seem unreasonable to me, and I may reject it as constituting no part of the revelation. For the same reason, my neighbor may reject an-other passage. In this way, the whole Bible may be rejected, while it is professedly received.[3]

Though neither the degree nor partial theory could marshal explicit biblical sanction, the partial theorists did claim Scriptural support for their side, and this troubled high view advocates. The Bible, partial theorists asserted, contained within itself the very seeds of evidence for their po-sition in the form of disagreements between biblical writers, false state-ments made about matters of history and science, and clear discrepancies

2. Dick, *Inspiration of Holy Scriptures*, 28.

3. Pond, "Inspiration," 53.

between the sacred penmen and secular historians. Mistakes such as these tacitly supported the partial theory its adherents maintained. These and other doubts about the veracity of the Scripture incited a vigorous rebuttal in which the conservatives sought to silence their critics.

The manner in which high view advocates sought to answer their partial theory antagonists illustrates their commitment to inerrancy and their unwillingness to brook the existence of even one genuine error of any kind in the sacred volume. Specifically, partial theorists challenged inerrancy on several broad fronts: (1) in what sense could the high view claim full inspiration for the Bible since it contained internal contradictions and mistakes; and (2) how could the inerrancy of the Bible be maintained when it clearly conflicted with secular advances in knowledge. These weighty questions demanded sober reflection and measured response.[4]

The Bible and Internal Discrepancies

The allegation that the biblical writers contradicted each other constituted a most serious charge, one which, if left unanswered, would seriously impair the theory of inerrancy. The conservative forces, therefore, responded to this challenge directly. It is of no small consequence to note that appeal to the original autographs was a familiar tactic among the strict view theorists. Conservative scholars, seeking to qualify the attacks of the critics, insisted that their complaints be leveled against the reading of the original manuscripts rather than upon that of a corrupt copy. Any legitimate criticism had to be aimed at the reading of the original autographs, they argued.

This is plain in Woods' response to the critic's charges of discrepancies and disagreements between and among different biblical writers. Since the conservatives believed that the Holy Spirit authored the Bible, in all its parts, right down to the very words, they could not tolerate even one genuine contradiction. Realizing this, Woods wrote,

> Instances of apparent disagreement among different writers of the sacred volume, and of apparent contradiction in the same writers, are no valid objection against their inspiration. We often find that an appearance of contradiction vanishes on inquiry. . . . But suppose there are some instances in which we are unable to remove all appearance of contradiction. . . . Still we cannot decide with safety against the inspired writers; because farther inquiry, more information, and a better method of interpreting the sacred writers, may help us discover a consistency which at present does not appear.

4. Some excerpts from pages 25–33 appear in Satta, "Inerrancy," 79–96.

> And, if, in some instances, we find it necessary to admit, that in the *present copies* of the Scriptures there are real contradictions; even this cannot be relied on as proof, that the original writers were not divinely inspired; because these contradictions may be owing to the mistakes of transcribers. And it is very well known, that the most remarkable instances of contradiction are found in those words or sentences, in which a mistake in copying might have been most easily made. And considering how the Scriptures abound with details of names, numbers, and facts, and minute circumstances, it would seem to be a matter of wonder, that the copyists committed no more mistakes, rather than they committed so many.[5]

Opponents believed incongruities between and among the synoptic gospel writers made inerrancy vulnerable. Critics marshaled many instances in which the biblical writers seemed to disagree. For instance one "insuperable problem" concerned the hour of Christ's passion. The gospel of Mark appeared to disagree with the gospel of John regarding this pivotal event. According to Mark, Jesus was already crucified at "the third hour" or at nine o'clock in the morning (Mark 15:25). However, John asserts that at "about the sixth hour" Pilate was still in consultation as to what to do with Christ (John 19:14). William Lee, in attempting to harmonize these two accounts, stated,

> It has been reserved for modern times to suggest a solution which has been almost universally accepted, and which removes every

---

5. Woods, *Lectures*, 35–36. In point of fact the inerrancy of the original autograph doctrine was exceedingly common among scholars throughout the nineteenth-century. It pervades the literature. Theologians regularly assumed that only the sacred writers produced inspired writ, so that only the first edition text was considered inerrant being "God-breathed." Biblical scholars took this proposition as one of the rudimentary principles of textual analysis. Eleazar Lord is representative of this outlook, writing, "That the words of the original text of Scripture, being the words in which the Divine thoughts were inspired into the minds of the sacred writers, infallibly represent those thoughts, and are as infallible as the thoughts are. . . . The Divine act of inspiration conveyed the thoughts which the Scriptures express, to the minds of the sacred writers. . . . It conveyed those thoughts in words—in the words which they were at the same time moved to speak and write. The Spirit spake by them. His word was on their tongue. . . . The Divine act of inspiration, rendered the sacred writers infallible in respect to what they received, and wrote in their official character. What they received they wrote. What they received was the infallible word of God. What they wrote, therefore, was his infallible word. . . . The sacred writers were persons specially selected to be the organs through whom what was inspired into their minds was to be communicated and written, and thereby to constitute the Holy Scriptures. Such were the prophets and apostles whose office in relation to this subject, it was to speak and write the words of God conveyed to them by inspiration." Lord, *Inspiration, not Guidance nor Intuition*, 16, 35, 39.

shade of difficulty from the case. . . . The explanation for this apparent discordance in time . . . is, that S. John has given the hour
according to the Roman calculation of time, which counted as we
do, from midnight; while S. Mark adheres to the Jewish custom of
counting from sunrise.[6]

By applying this reasoning, the two accounts, rather than conflicting,
corresponded, providing a window of time in which Pilate assessed his
options (at six o'clock) leading up to the actual events of the crucifixion
(at around nine o'clock).

Another case that Lee considered pertained to the inscription records
over the cross. Partial theorists had long complained that the four gospel
historians hopelessly differed in their presentation of what Pilate wrote
above the head of Christ on the cross. In the account of Matthew it is stated that the inscription read, "This is Jesus the King of the Jews." However,
in Mark the writing was condensed to read "The King of the Jews." Luke
submits to the sacred volume a reading of "This is the King of the Jews,"
while John the apostle asserts that the title read, "Jesus of Nazareth the
King of the Jews."

Though at first blush discrepancies appear to exist, Lee argued that
such was not the case. Lee observed that the sacred penmen at no point
contradicted each other, noting that each wrote a portion of the inscription which was best suited to their purposes. The entire inscription, Lee asserted, must have read, "This is Jesus of Nazareth the King of the Jews." If
this reading is accepted, no contradiction among the gospel writers exists.
Rather, each one recorded that which accomplished his purposes while
contributing to the full reading of the title.[7]

Not every challenge could be answered so succinctly. However, Lee
argued that if *any* means existed to harmonize a biblical account, this was
always preferable to admitting a genuine discrepancy. After all, he argued,
history is replete with illustrations of how one fortunate discovery clarified
what appeared to be an irreconcilable variance between records and writers.[8] Thus the sacred writers should always receive the benefit of the doubt,
even in cases of apparent genuine discrepancies.

6. Lee, *Inspiration of Holy Scripture*, 351–52.

7. Ibid.

8. Lee offers this insight from secular history, "The medals struck for the coronation of
Louis XIV gave a different day from that which all contemporary historians agree in fixing
for the date of the event. Of all these writers only one has noticed a circumstance which
accounts for this discrepancy: for he alone mentions that the coronation had been appointed to take place on the day given by the medals—which were accordingly prepared—but

Another common textual inconsistency existed regarding numbers. For instance, critics alleged that Stephen made an error recorded in Acts 7:14, when he noted that the number of Jacob's family that traveled into Egypt totaled seventy-five. This, they asserted, conflicted with statements made by Moses in Gen 46:26 and 27. Moses as well seemed to contradict himself by stating first that the number was sixty-six and then seventy. How could one reconcile these differing enumerations?

The answer rested in the manner in which family lines were delineated. Enoch Pond harmonized the Mosaic account by first counting only the lineal descendants of Jacob, those who, according to the biblical writer, "came forth from his loins" (Gen 46:26). By subtracting Jacob himself and Joseph and his two sons (who were already in Egypt), the number is sixty-six. By adding these four back in according to the phraseology of verse 27, which reads "all the souls of the house of Jacob, which came into Egypt" one arrives at the number seventy. But what of the count rendered by Stephen?

If Jacob, Joseph, and his two sons are excluded from the list, and the number of Jacob's sons' wives is included—the number reaches seventy-five. "And that the sons' wives were included in the reckoning of Stephen is evident from his language. 'All his *kindred* were threescore and fifteen souls.' The sons' wives, surely, were in the number of Jacob's 'kindred,' though they were not his lineal descendents."[9]

Another case of discrepant numbers occurred in recounting the number of people who died in Israel due to fornicating with the daughters of Midian. In this case, Moses asserts that twenty-four thousand people died of the plague (Num 25:9), while Paul states that only twenty-three thousand perished (1 Cor 10:8). However, this apparent disagreement found a resolution in the following explanation:

> Before the plague broke out, God commanded Moses to take the leaders in this wickedness, and hang them up before the Lord. In the execution of this order, as many as a thousand, in all probability, perished. These Moses included in the number of those who fell, while Paul refers only to those who died of the plague.[10]

---

that circumstances caused a delay till the date assigned by the historians. Nothing could be simpler than this: and yet in a thousand years, had no such explanation been given, antiquarians would have been sadly perplexed in their efforts to reconcile the contradiction." Lee, *Inspiration*, 363.

9. Pond, "Alleged Discrepancies in the Bible," 382–93.

10. Ibid., 393.

The detailed and exacting manner in which conservative scholars scrutinized, assessed, and answered alleged contradictions serves to illuminate their devotion to an error-free composition. Biblical writers could never contradict one another, nor could biblical numbers fail to agree, because God, who authored the text, could never speak in anything other than complete and utter harmony.

Nor did they consider it possible for the biblical writers to conflict when discussing doctrinal issues, most especially redemptive matters—the apex of biblical revelation. Scripture spoke in complete accord when addressing salvation. Partial theorists, on the other hand, pointed to the discrepancies of doctrine presented by the apostle Paul and James. James, they argued, made salvation a matter of works, while Paul endorsed salvation by faith in Christ alone. They portrayed Paul and James as at irreconcilable loggerheads. However, the conservatives decried such notions, arguing that when interpreted in context, the alleged disparity between them disappeared. In a lengthy rebuttal against the critics, one theologian responded,

> "Ye see then, how that by works a man is justified, and not by faith only" (James 2:24); "Therefore we conclude that a man is justified by faith without the deeds of the law" (Rom. 3:28); these two texts have often been arrayed, like hostile combatants, against each other. But is there between them any more discrepancy than between the two following of Paul: "Not the hearers of the law are just before God, but the doers of the law shall be justified"; "A man is justified by faith without the deeds of the law." In the latter case the commentators rightly reconcile these different, and apparently contradictory statements, by a consideration of the different objects which the apostle had in view. Like every other writer of good sense, he adapts, they tell us, his language to the case in hand. If he is discussing the question of the *meritorious ground* of forgiveness and justification, he tells us that man is justified by faith, without the deeds of the law. But if the question is: *What course of moral conduct* is acceptable to God? He affirms that "not the hearers of the law are just before God, but the doers of the law shall be justified." A good and sufficient explanation this. Now let the same just canon of interpretation be applied to the language of James as compared with that of Paul, and the alleged discrepancy vanishes.[11]

In other words, advocates of inerrancy argued that when the context of a given writer was assessed carefully, apparent contradictions often harmonized. A judicious analysis of both Paul and James demonstrated an

---

11. Barrows, "Alleged Disagreement between Paul and James," 768–69.

accord between them, agreeing that salvation was indeed by faith in Christ alone. James stressed the consequences and proofs of genuine faith while Paul emphasized the actual mechanism of redemption. Thus whether pertaining to matters of facts, figures, or faith, the conservatives would not capitulate; arguing for complete internal harmony of the biblical text. But what did they say about disparities alleged between the Scripture and advances in secular knowledge, most especially in history and geology? Whose authority reigned preeminent—that of science or the Bible?

The Bible and History/Geography

Advocates of the high view of inspiration believed that Scripture was historically and geographically accurate in every detail—even including apparently incidental events. The true facts of secular history would always corroborate the veracity of the word of God, they asserted, and indeed, asserted confidently.

The history of the Jews from the divided monarchy, constantly attested to by outside sources, is but one example. The separate existence of Judah and Israel, the wars in which they engaged against their neighbors, the invasion of Shishak king of Egypt, and Zerah the Ethiopian, and the repeated aggression between Ahab and Benhadad all received verification by external sources. The names of the monarchs reigning over Babylon during the captivity were even etched in the region's building materials. "The plain of Babylon has one voice . . . the *inscribed bricks,* used as they are for all edifices . . . still show from whence they came, and they all tell who was the mighty monarch who raised the buildings of Babylon: the inscription on each is, Nebuchadnezzar, son of Nabopolassar."[12]

They considered secular historians less reliable than the sacred writers—who wrote under divine guidance. Even if profane sources seemed to contradict a biblical account, theologians encouraged restraint in concluding against the biblical writer, noting that new discoveries might well clear away the alleged discrepancy. For instance, William Lee gave an important historical note on just such an occurrence.

In Dan 5:30 the text records the death of Belshazzar the king of the Chaldeans on the night of the invasion of Babylon by the Medo-Persian forces commanded by Cyrus. However, the name Belshazzar was not attested to by any secular sources. Indeed, historians depicted the event in a very different manner than the biblical writer, omitting any mention of Belshazzar.

12. Robinson, "Rawlinson's Historical Evidences," 510–11.

Josephus, arguing from a fragment of Berosus, places Nabonnedus as the last king of Babylon. Upon hearing of the invasion, Nabonnedus assembled forces to oppose the occupation but was overwhelmed and defeated. Receiving clemency at the hands of Cyrus, Nabonnedus received a settlement in Carmania, where he later died. Nabonnedus (with some spelling variations) is declared as the last king of Babylon by a number of other historians as well. This fact appeared to confute the historical accuracy of the Bible which assigned the monarchy to Belshazzar.

However, an important discovery by Rawlinson in 1854 had apparently removed the discrepancy. Lee noted,

> A number of clay cylinders have been lately disinterred in the ruins of Um-Qeer (the ancient Ur of the Chaldees), two of which contain a memorial of the works executed by Nabonidus (the last king of Babylon) in southern Chaldaea. The most important fact which they disclose is, that the eldest son of Nabonidus was named Bel-shar-ezar, and that he was admitted by his father to share in the government. This name is undoubtedly the Belshazzar . . . of Daniel, and thus furnishes us with *a key to the explanation of that great historical problem which has hitherto defied solution.* We can now understand how Belshazzar, as joint king with his father, may have been governor of Babylon, when the city was attacked by the combined forces of the Medes and Persians, and may have perished in the assault that followed; while Nabonidus, leading a force to the relief of the place, was defeated, and obliged to take refuge in the neighboring town of Borsippa, capitulating, after a short resistance, and being subsequently assigned, according to Berosus, an honorable retirement in Carmania. By the discovery, indeed, of the name of Bel-shar-ezar, as appertaining to the son of Nabonidus, we are, for the first time, enabled to reconcile authentic history with the inspired record of Daniel.[13]

High view advocates believed that the Bible offered exacting, precise information on historical events. They affirmed the absolute reliability of Scripture whenever it spoke to events, persons, places, or customs. They considered everything of a historical nature addressed by Scripture completely true, and in fact, defended as true all historical details against any charges of prevarication, confusion, or error on the part of the inspired penmen.[14]

13. Lee, *Inspiration*, 349.

14. Not only was the historicity of the Old Testament vigorously defended, but that of the New as well. A minute detail offered by Luke is defended with equal degrees of tenacity, as Lee writes, "S. Luke in the thirteenth chapter gives the title of Proconsul to the Governor

Not only did the strict view advocates contend that the Bible was perfect in its historical depictions, but they also argued that its discussions on matters pertaining to geography also exhibited divine insight and authority. For instance, one scholar pointed to the eye witness account given by Abraham of the divine judgment of Sodom and Gomorrah, arguing that the topography of the region fully corroborated his description. The biblical account informs the reader that Abraham dwelt near Hebron when the judgment fell. Following the catastrophe, the text goes on to state that Abraham looked toward the site (now charred to ashes) and "beheld the smoke of the country as the smoke of a furnace (Genesis 19:28)."

The writer, assessing the locale of Hebron in connection to Sodom, contended that the Pentateuch received full confirmation in its testimony, stating,

> From the height which overlooks Hebron, where Abraham stood
> . . . the observer at the present day has an extensive view spread
> out before him towards the Dead Sea. The hills of Moab, sloping
> down towards that sea on the east, and a part of Idumea, are all
> in sight. A cloud of smoke rising from the plain would be visible
> to a person at Hebron now, and could have been, therefore, to
> Abraham, as he looked towards Sodom on the morning after its
> destruction by Jehovah.[15]

---

of Cypress. In this division, however, of the Roman Empire by Augustus, this island had been reserved for his own jurisdiction: and consequently its Governor must have borne the rank of Procurator;—that of Proconsul being appropriated to those who ruled the provinces which the Emperor had ceded to the Senate. The title here assigned by S. Luke to Sergius Paulus had for a long time perplexed commentators; who knew not how to reconcile the statement of the sacred historian with the assumed facts of the case. Some coins, however, were found bearing the effigy of the Emperor Claudius; and in the centre of the reverse occurs the word Cypress, while the surrounding legend gives the title in question of Proconsul to an individual who must have been the immediate successor or predecessor of Sergius Paulus. In addition to this evidence, a passage has been pointed out in the writings of Dio Cassius who mentions that Augustus, subsequently to his original settlement, had changed Cyprus and Gallia Narbonensis into Senatorial Provinces; the historian adding, as if with the design of establishing S. Luke's accuracy, 'And so it came to pass, that Proconsuls began to be sent to these nations also.' Had the writings of Dio Cassius perished . . . and the coins alluded to never been found, we should unquestionably, have seen this hypothetical blunder of the inspired historian foremost among the array of cases adduced by such writers as Strauss. Is not the Christian Apologist therefore fully justified in deprecating the precipitancy of criticism? Has he not ample grounds for maintaining that difficulties, such as those which we have considered, arise from our ignorance of the whole case; and that we have good reason to expect that they eventually will disappear as similar evidence accumulates." Lee, *Inspiration*, 363–64.

15. "Geographical Accuracy of the Bible," 452.

This author considered geographical precision crucial in vindicating biblical integrity regarding spiritual matters. If, he reasoned, Scripture turned out false in that which could be tested, what guarantee was there of its fidelity in matters of religion which could not be tested? He noted, "Suppose travelers now had returned from the East, saying that the region of the Dead Sea is not visible from the neighborhood of Hebron . . . what a shock would this give to our confidence in the Bible!"[16] If the biblical writers exhibited ignorance regarding these mundane affairs, what assurances existed that they were not equally flawed regarding matters of the soul?

These theologians expected Scripture to speak truthfully upon every matter it addressed—if it failed to do so, even once, their belief in its divine origin would suffer. They often pointed out tiny details in Scripture, sometimes centering on the truthfulness of a single word, which testified to its perfect accuracy. In the parable of the Good Samaritan, the Bible states that a certain man was going *down* from Jerusalem to Jericho and was assaulted by thieves (Luke 10:31). One theologian pointed out that Jericho actually rested in a valley about four thousand feet lower than Jerusalem. A traveler would in fact descend nearly the entire way from Jerusalem until reaching the plains of Jericho—exactly, he noted, as the Bible stated.

Furthermore, "The mode of describing the inverse journey from Jericho to Jerusalem is equally exact. Having crossed the Jordan from the eastern side, Jesus, as we read in Luke 19:28 and Mark 10:32 'went before' the disciples, 'ascending up to Jerusalem.'"[17] This illustration reveals how the integrity of the biblical account hinged on the accuracy of two descriptive words "up" and "down."

These small details could not fail to correspond to the actual geography of the ancient world, because the Holy Spirit directed the writing process, producing a composition entirely without error. These scholars considered the Bible internally harmonious and historically and geographically consistent with the strictest standards of reliability and accuracy.[18] However, their sturdiest challenge arose from the emerging science of geology, which posed a serious threat to the inviolability of the sacred text.

16. Ibid.

17. Ibid., 463.

18. The vigorous discourse regarding biblical inerrancy throughout the first five decades of the nineteenth-century makes the assertion of evangelical historian Mark Noll suspect, implying as he does that biblical literalism did not flourish until the end of the nineteenth-century. The lively antebellum discussion among scholars devoted to such matters seems to contradict this suggestion. Noll, *Scandal of the Evangelical Mind*, 124.

The Bible and Geology

No advances in secular knowledge posed a more daunting challenge to the inerrant view than did the development of geological science in the early nineteenth-century. From the study of the earth's crust and its layers, scientists speculated that the earth must have been very old—many millions of years old. This conflicted with the literal rendering of the Genesis account whereby many theologians had dated the age of the earth and all its inhabitants at around 6,000 years old. Some geologists attempted to build a bridge between these two apparently antipodal theories, demonstrating in the process that a commitment to inerrancy was not a position exclusively relegated to theologians.

Edward Hitchcock, eminent professor of chemistry and later President of Amherst College, wrote profusely on this issue. A series of his articles on geology and the Bible appeared in the *Biblical Repository* from 1835–1838. While Hitchcock believed that advances in science could improve one's understanding of the Bible, he affirmed the integrity of the biblical record, noting that when rightly interpreted the Bible spoke accurately in every detail. In discussing the connection between geology and the Mosaic cosmogony in the Bible, Hitchcock endorsed the high view of Scripture in the first of his contributions to the *Repository*,

> If they both proceed from the infinitely perfect being, there cannot be any real discrepancy between them. So that if we discover any apparent disagreement, we either do not rightly understand geology, or we give a wrong interpretation to the Scriptures, or the Bible is not true. We hope to show to the satisfaction of every reasonable and candid mind, that we are by no means compelled to adopt the last of these conclusions.[19]

This first article, devoted to describing ways in which geology and Scripture agreed, sought to mitigate the alleged conflict between them. Hitchcock noted a number of ways in which the Bible and geology har-

19. Hitchcock, "Connection between Geology and the Mosaic History of the Creation," 442. Hitchcock was not alone in his conviction that nature and Scripture would always harmonize due to their singular divine source. God, the creator of both, could never contradict himself. As another scholar noted, "If geology is true, it must agree with the Scriptures, rightly interpreted. The God of nature and the God of revelation is one." Cutting "Geology and Religion," 382. And another theologian confidently declared ". . . we can never be made to believe, by any course of reasoning however plausible, that there is a single fact of a scientific nature that conflicts with revelation. That there may seem to be a collision need not be denied; but that there is a real collision we can never admit." Dana, "Religion of Geology," 519.

monized: they both agreed that the universe, created out of nothing, had a beginning, they both affirmed that fire and water functioned as the two catalytic agents in affecting change on the globe since creation, both acknowledged that the continents of the globe had at one time been submerged (that a deluge as the one described by Moses had occurred in the not too distant past), they both testified to the progressive nature of creation, they also both asserted that humans had only recently come upon the earth, and finally both records agreed that the world would eventually be destroyed by fire.[20] He concluded by contending that through geology one derives "presumptive evidence in favor of the sacred historian."[21]

Some six months after the first journal article appeared, Hitchcock submitted another lengthy essay (71 pages) in which he once again sought to reconcile alleged discrepancies between geology and revelation. In doing so, he adamantly affirmed his faith in the full inspiration of the Bible. He set forth fourteen different interpretations of the Mosaic history of creation. The first two represented the position of skeptics or unbelievers who, Hitchcock asserted, regarded the facts of Scripture as fables—merely the misinformed opinions of fallible people. In refuting such ideas Hitchcock stated,

> This view of the subject so evidently aims a death blow at the plenary inspiration of the Scriptures, that it would seem we need spend little time in its refutation. For, if one may pronounce the chronological and scientific facts given in the Bible to be uninspired, another man may select any other facts which seem to him opposed to philosophy and right reason, and reject them as uninspired; and so on, until nothing is left of the word of God which is opposed to human prejudice and corruption. True, it was not the object of the Bible to instruct in philosophy: but moral truth as stated in the Scriptures is connected with physical truth; and until the sacred writers inform us that they were inspired as to the one but not as to the other, we have no right to pronounce them infallible as to the one, but liable to error as to the other.[22]

For Hitchcock, diminishing the inspired status of the factual assertions of the Bible denied inspiration altogether. Hitchcock viewed Scripture as authoritative in both matters of faith and matters of fact—even extend-

---

20. Ibid., 443–51.

21. Ibid., 451.

22. Hitchcock, "Connection between Geology and the Mosaic History of the Creation," (October 1835): 270.

ing to scientific issues. This is not to say that Hitchcock thought the Bible spoke in strictly scientific language, for he did not.

Scripture was addressed to the common person, and since no one in the ancient world possessed familiarity with the scientific discoveries of the nineteenth-century, it made little sense for the sacred writers to speak in the parlance of modern scientific thought. However, though not a scientific textbook, neither would the Bible, when fairly interpreted, ever confute or contradict the rightly interpreted facts of science. Science and Scripture would always complement one another never contradict each other, he believed.[23]

In order to explain the earth's ancient age, which, based on the assumption of uniformitarianism, Hitchcock surmised extended many millions of years, he employed the "gap" theory. This hypothesis sought to rescue revealed religion from disparagement by providing a holding-bin between Gen 1:1 and 1:2 for the storage of the many millions of years which geologists urged were required to explain the formation of the geologic column. In Gen 1:1, Hitchcock argued, Moses simply declared that God made the universe. A lengthy gap ensued between that declaration and verse 2 in which Moses resumed the story of how God filled this world with its present inhabitants, taking six literal days to accomplish and occurring some six thousand years ago.[24]

Significantly Hitchcock argued in favor of this idea by asserting that it did no violence to the language of the text—he went so far as to say "It seems to us that this is precisely the impression that would be made upon a plain unlettered man of good sense from a perusal of this chapter without any previous bias."[25] While he asserted that science could shed valuable light onto the correct interpretation of the Bible, Hitchcock never intimated that Scripture ever erred—his solution argued the other way—offering a remedy in which the language of the Bible retained its integrity

---

23. Ibid., 270. Geology, considered a callow newcomer at this time, held a decidedly subordinate place against Scripture in the minds of the conservatives. One of the elite, spanking a young geologist who dared suggest a more prominent role for geological inquiry warned, "If he [Miller] may set aside the plain and indubitable grammatical sense of a passage because it does not accord with his geology, the astronomer, the physiologist, the archaeologist, the rationalistic metaphysician, may set aside any other passage or passages, because it does not accord with the theories they entertain of their favorite branches of knowledge. Mr. Miller's persuasion that geology has become a science, and that its conclusions are authoritative, is no more a justification for his course [reinterpreting Genesis], than the like persuasion of rationalists and atheists is of theirs." Lord, "Two Records," 129.

24. Ibid., 314–15.

25. Ibid., 317.

and veracity. Hitchcock, endorsing biblical authority over that of science, stated, "So strong is the proof of the authenticity and inspiration of the sacred record, that even if *point blank* inconsistency could be made out between it and geology, the latter must yield, because it is not sustained by proof so strong as revelation."[26]

The following spring found Hitchcock fending off charges of heresy leveled by Professor Moses Stuart of Andover (who like Woods endorsed the high view of inspiration) for promoting unorthodox views of biblical interpretation. Hitchcock once again asserted his adherence to the inerrancy of the Bible, but reaffirmed his belief that science could open new avenues of interpretive insight, assisting the theologian in his work.

He reminded his readers that it was scarcely 200 years prior that the Christian world, almost unanimously, believed that the sun, moon, and stars revolved around the stationary earth. Advances of modern science, precipitating the Copernican revolution, had assisted philologists in understanding that Moses had employed the language of phenomenon in stating that the sun rose and set.[27] Why could not science continue assisting exegetes in their labors?

Moreover he argued that geology affirmed the biblical testimony of the Noachian flood, proving it a friend of revealed religion. In both 1837 and 1838 Hitchcock noted that empirical evidence existed promoting the idea of a flood of great—if not universal—extent. Arguing from the position of boulders and diluvial gravel found in an almost uniformly southerly direction and from scratches on stationary rocks running nearly constantly north and south, Hitchcock asserted that evidence for a powerful deluge existed in the geologic evidence.[28]

In considering the possibility that the Genesis flood was one of great extent rather than a world-wide catastrophe, Hitchcock took pains to consider the latitude afforded to the interpreter due to the language of the account. He agreed that at the initial reading the words appeared decisive in favor of a universal cataclysm. However, upon closer inspection, he asserted that "The Jews have well observed that . . . *all, every* is not to be

26. Ibid., 327. It was widely perceived by the theological elite that good science would in fact always buttress the assertions of the Bible. "There can be no doubt that the two lights, science and revelation, instead of being set up as rivals, can be so arranged that their flames shall coalesce and form one which shall be of greater splendor than either of them alone. Science may thus become the handmaid of religion, assisting her in obtaining conquests over the minds and hearts of men." Dana, "Religion of Geology," 505.

27. Hitchcock, "Remarks on Professor Stuart's Examination of Gen. 1," 452–53.

28. Hitchcock, "Historical and Geological Deluges Compared," 336, 353.

understood, on all occasions, with the mathematical sense of *all*; because it is also used to signify *many*."[29] Hitchcock maintained that the words of Scripture permitted interpreting the flood account as constituting a deluge of great extent, though localized, rather than demanding a world wide cataclysm.

However, he conceded that if the language of Moses meant that the ark actually settled upon the summit of present day Mount Ararat in Armenia, and that the waters rose fifteen additional cubits above that region "we can hardly conceive it possible that so mighty a wave should not sweep over the whole globe, either in its flux or reflux."[30] In seeking to support his localized flood theory, Hitchcock again appealed to the language of the text, arguing that the words of Moses did not demand that the ark rested at the highest peak on the mountains, even allowing that perhaps a different mountain range was in view.[31]

Writing twenty five years after his first article appeared in the *Biblical Repository*, Hitchcock, then President of Amherst College, continued to affirm the reliability and veracity of the biblical record. He continued to endorse the gap theory as an explanation for the old earth and the development of the geologic column of the earth's crust.

Though he intimated that the days of Genesis might be metaphorical in some sense, as permitted by the language, he continued to affirm their literalness personally. Endeavoring to retain the integrity of the biblical accounts, he argued that though not a scientific textbook, the Bible taught highly accurate information about creation, receiving corroboration by science.

Acutely aware of the sometimes foreboding aura precipitated by the encroachments of geologic science upon Scripture, he offered words of

29. Hitchcock, "Historical and Geological Deluges Compared," 6.

30. Ibid., 7.

31. Ibid., 8. That the actual language of Scripture was considered authoritative evidence in scientific dispute is clearly seen in this rebuttal of the Day Age theory. Regarding the literal six day theory one scholar noted, "It is not advanced as a hypothesis that the Mosaic record indubitably affirms that the creation of the heavens and earth was accomplished in the period of six natural days about six thousand years ago. To advance it as an hypothesis would imply that there is no direct and specific affirmation that the creation took place in the six days. But that is not what the parties to whom he refers maintain [those who endorse a literal six day creation]. They hold . . . that the narrative in Genesis "indubitably" teaches that the creation of the heavens and earth was wrought in the six days, and they show that no other construction can be put on the language of the record. . . . It is the natural grammatical meaning of the passage, which they receive and maintain as the truth." Lord, "On the Relation between the Holy Scriptures, and Some Parts of Geological Science," 610.

comfort and support for those committed to the truthful character of the Bible. Reflecting on the changes he had witnessed over a scientific career spanning over thirty years, Hitchcock stated,

> From all that has been advanced we may safely say, that no other science, nay, perhaps not all the sciences, touch religion at so many points as geology . . . If upon a few of them [points] some obscurity still rests, yet with nearly all how clear the harmony—how strong the mutual corroboration! With how much stronger faith do we cling to the Bible when we find so many of its principles thus corroborated! . . . Surely it is time that unbelievers, like the ancient heathen, should confess the divinity of the Bible, when they see how invulnerable it is to every assault. Surely it is time for the believer to cease fearing that any deadly influence will emanate from geology and fasten itself upon his faith, and learn to look upon this science only as an auxiliary and friend.[32]

Not only were some men of science such as Hitchcock endorsing amity between profane and sacred knowledge, many theologians expressed similar opinions. One of the most significant features of the book by William Lee on inspiration was his commitment to answering the objections of the critics. Investing over fifty pages of his book to systematically respond to three critical complaints leveled against the inerrancy doctrine, his third rebuttal concentrated on the alleged collision between science and the testimony of Scripture.

Some biblical statements had become literal land mines. The book of Joshua, for instance, declared that the sun stood still, and numerous writers, including Jesus, referred to the sun rising and setting, etc. These statements, some urged, were contradictory to fact and hence could not be inspired. How could deity have made such obvious blunders? However, Lee refused to admit any genuine contradiction between the biblical records and scientific data.[33]

Arguing that the writers of Scripture could have made use of only one of two languages; the language of the senses or that of science, Lee endorsed the complete validity of the phenomenal form of expression they selected. He attempted to sustain his argument by noting that the language of science would have been contrary to their purposes, being unintelligible to a primitive audience.

32. Hitchcock, "Religion of Geology," 709.

33. Lee, *Inspiration*, 367.

Science, he asserted, creates new language as new discoveries are made and theories generated, but the language of the senses remains the same. Thus, he argued, it possesses inherent advantages over the more technical language of science. He wrote, "The only language which is fixed is that of ordinary life; whereby the phenomena are described as they appear to the senses."[34]

In his work Lee made a distinction between revelation and inspiration, noting that the former represented divine dictation, as would be necessary in prophetic writing. All the literature in the Bible was inspired (or so guided and controlled by the Holy Spirit that every part was without error), but not the entire inspired product was revelatory. Scientists wrongly balked against some statements of Scripture, he contended, believing that they were meant to represent divine dictation in the relaying of scientific information. Actually, however, the accounts represented a faithful retelling of a historic event related as "a reliable eye-witness must have related it."[35] The divine intention was to communicate with not to confuse the hearers, as Lee noted, "The sacred historian, consequently, has drawn up his narrative, as a narrative of facts can only be drawn up, in the language of those for whom he writes."[36]

Lee encouraged the vigorous pursuit of scientific and philosophical knowledge. People of faith need never fear such pursuits, he asserted. For in fact, good science and philosophy would only confirm the testimony of the word of God. In concluding his work, Lee expressed confidence in the harmonious consequences of sincere inquiry, writing,

> No one truth can be contradictory to any other truth. The question which we must settle in the first instance, and on its own peculiar evidence, is—Does the Bible come from God? And if it be Divine (and therefore true), "then is it certain, demonstrably certain—that no fact in the universe—in heaven above, or earth beneath, or in the waters or rocks under the earth—can possibly be really inconsistent with it."[37]

If the received interpretation of a passage of Scripture appeared contradictory to the alleged facts of scientific discovery, theologians needed to respond to this inconsistency. Lee argued that they must ". . . examine how

34. Ibid., 368.

35. Ibid., 371.

36. Ibid., 369.

37. Ibid., 374. Lee stated, "I here avail myself of the very forcible argument of the writer in the 'Christian Remembrancer' *loc. Cit.*, pp. 232–4."

this discrepancy is to be set right, and to teach in what other way the face of the world and the words of God may be shown to be—as when rightly understood, they must, of necessity be—perfectly harmonious."[38]

The conservative response to the challenge of their critics was systematic and thorough, consistently defending the inerrant quality of the original autographs, while arguing that everything the Bible asserted, whether pertaining to matters of faith or matters of fact was necessarily perfect—down to the very words. They attempted to show that a complete harmony existed among the biblical writers, reconciling alleged discrepancies through a variety of means—not least of which included an appeal to the original autographs of Scripture. Biblical authority extended well beyond the borders of faith, staking its claim on the secular realms of history, geography, and science, most especially the emerging study of geology.

Though the biblical writers, they alleged, spoke in the language of sense rather than the language of science, the Bible, when interpreted correctly, would never fail to correspond to the true findings of all secular investigation. How could the author of both the word and the world be in conflict? Thus the adherents of the high view sought to defend the integrity of the biblical record and uphold its complete authority regarding every issue, whether secular or sacred, to which it spoke. Unfortunately, for the proponents of the strict theory, science would not long remain so amicable. In the decades to come advances in knowledge would incite increasing antipathy to the doctrine of inerrancy of the original autographs—the majority opinion regarding biblical authority throughout the first six decades of the nineteenth-century.

38. Lee, *Inspiration*, 374.

3

The High View Under Siege

Biblical Authority and Inspiration, 1860–1900

THE last four decades of the nineteenth-century, for concerned proponents of the high view, represented a season of increasing uncertainty
and unrelenting challenge. Geological science coupled with Darwinian
evolution theory exacerbated the already vexing questions regarding biblical authority and the world's cosmogony and human development. While
Darwinism did not necessarily imply atheism, it made it (and agnosti-
cism) intellectually respectable. The rise of theological liberalism, a blend
of rationalism, romanticism, and higher textual criticism, further divided
religious groups, splintering denominational cohesion and complicating
the debates over biblical authority. If the affront to inerrancy in the first
half century was a zephyr, this "unholy" trinity represented the gale.

The Bible and Geology: A Continuing Debate

The high view of inspiration, which would remain ascendant throughout
the nineteenth-century, nonetheless suffered violent storms throughout
the last four decades of that period. In unrelenting waves, both the science
of geology and Darwinian evolution theory assailed the high view. This
is illustrated in regard to the Mosaic cosmogony as understood by geologists and biblical scholars. One might suppose that scientists would be the
principal antagonists regarding the biblical account of creation while theologians would maintain the accuracy of the Scripture. This, however, was
not always the case. As the century progressed, confidence in the details of
the sacred text waned among some members of both groups.

In 1867 C. H. Hitchcock, following in the illustrious steps of his father Edward, argued scientifically that the Genesis cosmogony fully agreed
with the facts of geology. Any discrepancies were misperceptions. Some

disparities between father and son are noticeable, however. For instance, whereas the elder Hitchcock had maintained that the days in Genesis represented actual twenty-four hour periods of time, the younger Hitchcock modified that position. He noted,

> The time-words in Genesis were intended to be understood as literal days, like those used by the prophets, till the age came when their proper meaning is understood. Then we perceive the meaning of the symbol, and become aware of a two-fold signification. And we are authorized to apply either meaning to the term . . .[1]

The days actually referred to geologic epochs according to the younger Hitchcock.

Edward Hitchcock had argued in the 1830s that all the time needed by geology could be provided by the "gap" between Gen 1:1 and 1:2. This alleged "holding bin" afforded geologists with their millions of years without doing violence to the text of Scripture, permitting the elder Hitchcock to argue in favor of a literal rendering of the days in Genesis. His son reneged on that position. This subtle shift in methodology and interpretation further indicates the pressure mounting against the literal and inerrant view.

Nonetheless, C. H. Hitchcock vigorously argued in favor of the biblical record as a reliable witness to the facts of creation which scientific findings fully substantiated. Offering a detailed analysis of the days of Genesis along with the scientific explanation of creation, Hitchcock submitted a harmony which fully supported the biblical record. Each "day," accordingly, represented a geologic period. He stated, "It will be noticed that the order of the events, both as respects the times of introduction and predominance in the geological columns, agrees with that in the scriptural account."[2] He further postulated that the heavenly bodies, divinely created, first offered light to the earth "probably not later than the Silurian period."[3]

Hitchcock fully embraced the scientific model and superimposed that account upon the biblical record. In doing so, however, he found complete accord. Yet, an interesting transposition had occurred, placing science at the forefront of inquiry, with Scripture serving as a supporting addendum. The Bible was still true, but only insofar as the language of the text possessed the elasticity to accommodate scientific discoveries. For some scientists geology now dictated the terms of agreement rather

1. C. H. Hitchcock, "Relation of Geology to Theology," 451.

2. Ibid., 438.

3. Ibid.

than Scripture. The reverse had been the case during Edward Hitchcock's tenure. Nonetheless, C. H. Hitchcock ably harmonized the two witnesses in such a way as to do justice to geology while also affirming the reliability of the Bible. He confidently asserted:

> (1) The order of events in the inorganic creation is the same. Neither record fixes the time of the beginning, and both present the same order of light, atmosphere, day and night, clouds, water, dry land, oceans, the appearance of the heavenly bodies, and most of these before plants. (2) The order of the introduction of organisms is the same. Both describe plants before animals, the marine lower forms before reptiles, birds and reptiles before mammals, and mammals last of all before man. The agreement is perfect. (3) Apparent discrepancy is removed . . . The work of creation was progressive with intervals of repose. There were five evenings when there was rest. We find similar periods of creative inactivity in the scientific record. These are the most prominent features in science. There were successive epochs of creation followed by long intervals of repose.[4]

In the case of C. H. Hitchcock, one finds a geologist laboring to corroborate the biblical account with scientific discoveries. By the end of the century, one encounters some liberal theologians abandoning the text of Scripture as hopelessly riddled with errors—incapable of rescue against the findings of science. Such was the case of S. R. Driver, a Hebrew scholar of no small renown.

Driver, Regius Professor of Hebrew, and Canon of Christ Church, Oxford produced, along with Francis Brown and Charles Briggs, what was and remains the definitive Hebrew Lexicon of the Old Testament.[5] An article he wrote which appeared in the *Sunday School Times* in December of 1886 created significant concerns among biblical conservatives. The cause of the consternation was his assertion that the Genesis account of creation differed substantially with the cosmogony taught by science. In a follow up article appearing in the *Andover Review* in 1887, Driver iterated this claim with greater detail and force. He argued:

> even after making every allowance for the popular, non-scientific phraseology of Genesis, I found it simply impossible honestly and straightforwardly to compare the record in Genesis with the record as taught by geology and astronomy, and to say that the two, even approximately, coincided. The records differed; and by no legitimate method or artifice which I had seen applied to

4. Ibid., 450–51.

5. Brown, Driver, and Briggs, *Hebrew and English Lexicon of the Old Testament*, 1905.

them could the differences be made to vanish, or even be shown to be insignificant.[6]

Ironically, Driver, a biblical scholar, argued against the reliability of the biblical account of creation based on the language of the text. He felt that harmonizers did an injustice to the words and grammar of the Bible in an effort to make it declare what it in fact did not say. While attempting to maintain the integrity of the Hebrew text, Driver willingly sacrificed its literal message as having little merit when juxtaposed against the teachings of science. He stated:

> But our only knowledge of the ideas which the sacred writers received is obtained from the language in which they have expressed them; and our only means of determining the sense which this is intended to convey is by observing attentively the usage of Scripture. Were the Hebrew words concerned of rare occurrence, or doubtful signification, were there any ambiguity of construction or sense, the latitude claimed would be cheerfully and cordially granted. But no such doubt or ambiguity exists. . . . I do not seek for discrepancies in the Biblical narrative; but where they exist, it seems to me that the only wise and right course in the Christian apologist is truthfully and fearlessly to acknowledge them.[7]

This illustration from geologic science provides important clues into the pressures mounting against the inerrant position as the century progressed. Edward Hitchcock the geologist, in the 1830s, had argued for the inerrancy of the biblical record "without any violence to the text." His

6. Driver, "Biblical and Historical Criticism," 639.

7. Ibid., 649. Of course, not all scientists or biblical scholars had adopted Driver's pessimism about biblical inerrancy as we shall see shortly. In battling against such conclusions, some biblical scholars and scientists had been pressed to accept the "Day Age theory" as a means to rebuttal. The Yale scholar James D. Dana is indicative of this course. In his response to the above article by S. R. Driver he wrote, "All geological interpretations assume . . . *that time was long* and *progress slow*; and if the "day" of Genesis is admitted to have exceeded the twenty-four hours, as it is now by many interpreters of the text, the second proposition, *progress was slow*, is sanctioned. The various significations of the word day in the Hebrew text, and other considerations, have gained from not a few theological writers this admission with regard to it. . . . The admission is equivalent, as I have said, to an acceptance of the proposition that progress was slow; and an acceptance, therefore, of the truths taught by nature as to the successive steps of progress; as to the order in the introduction of species of plants and animals; and as to a system of 'development' or 'evolution' in nature, if the study of nature establishes the fact of such a system . . . Slow progress was, beyond doubt, the fact of nature; and the question is: Does the chapter [Gen 1] also admit of, or favor, this interpretation? If it does, the harmony is all that could be desired." Dana, "On the Cosmogony of Genesis," 199.

modification suggested the existence of a gap between Gen 1:1 and 1:2. C. H. Hitchcock, writing in the 1860s, needed both the "gap" between Gen 1:1 and 1:2 and the "Day Age" theory in order to accommodate the findings of science with the biblical record. The elasticity of language was necessary to correlate the existing sacred and secular evidence. S. R. Driver, a biblical scholar, writing in the 1880s, sought to retain the integrity of the text, but in the process renounced any of its pretensions to scientific veracity.

For Driver, and other theological liberals, the Bible no longer functioned as the arbiter of truth. Its spiritual message was still esteemed. However, appealing to it in matters of history and science was no longer tenable, they urged. For them, the authority of science had usurped the authority of Scripture. Proponents of the high view of inspiration, as one might imagine, considered such concessions appalling. They had no intention of capitulating to the designs of such "low view" advocates, but stoutly responded, just as conservatives had done all along.

The Bible and Darwin

Another juggernaut against the conservative view of biblical authority emerged in 1859, steadily gaining momentum throughout the century. This new rival offered a paradigm which, if accepted, might effectively eclipse not only biblical authority, but a theistic worldview itself. Darwinism, as Charles Hodge incisively recognized early into the joust, represented a crucial test juxtaposing a God-centered universe with one devoid of design—nothing more than the product of chance and time.

That Darwinian gradualism presented a serious challenge to a theistic concept of the universe is axiomatic in our day. However, in nineteenth-century America theologians did not always assume such a jarring disjuncture between evolution theory and theism. Indeed, as we have observed, some theologians and geologists felt that the concepts associated with the gradual development of organisms by means of natural processes could be made to fit with biblical teaching, safeguarding biblical authority by introducing ideas such as the "gap" theory or the "Day Age" theory. So long as the language of Scripture possessed the resiliency to accommodate scientific theories postulating the age of the universe at millions rather than thousands of years, biblical authority was not entirely undercut by science.

However, Darwin made conservatives jittery—and with good reason. For while, many argued, an acceptance of Darwin's theory did not demand atheism, they knew it permitted it, making belief in a universe of blind chance intellectually respectable. The stark notion of a meaningless universe was the line of demarcation between Darwin and other theories of evolution. No conservative recognized this peril with greater perspicuity than did Charles Hodge of Princeton.

Though conservative theologians generally agreed that one could accept evolution and remain a committed theist, Hodge urged that no such amity could exist between theists and Darwinians. He made a stark contrast between "evolution" and Darwinian gradualism. Evolution, the belief that organisms gradually ascended from primitive to more complex life forms, frequently admitted the essential presence of God. Theistic evolutionists believed that the gradual development of organisms could only happen under the benevolent design of an all wise and powerful deity. Scripture could accommodate the protracted time periods required for such a model by appealing to the "gap" or "Day Age" theories.

Hodge, a contemporary of Darwin, was one of the first theologians to discriminate between evolution and Darwinism, contending that Darwin's theory represented a virulent attack against Christianity and the Bible. Hodge carefully analyzed Darwinism in his 1874 book, appropriately entitled, *What is Darwinism?* Written as an exposé, Hodge intended his book to reveal important subtleties of Darwin's theory that had the potential to poison and destroy biblical authority and Christianity if left unchecked.

Interestingly, Hodge asserted that Darwinism had but one thoroughly original contribution to make, noting that neither evolution proper nor natural selection represented this novelty. Indeed, Hodge noted that Darwin himself credited Lamarck with teaching, as early as 1811, that all species, including man have descended from other species.[8] Furthermore, Hodge argued that concepts pertaining to natural selection were found in earlier works as well, most especially in "The Vestiges of Creation" produced in 1844. The thing that set Darwin apart from other evolutionary models pertained to its obvious exclusion of a designer, Hodge contended. For Darwin postulated that all life emerged through the blind struggle for existence without any teleological purpose or divine guidance whatsoever. The absence of a designer, Hodge argued, was the truly significant contribution of Darwinism. Hodge stated:

> It is however neither evolution nor natural selection, which give Darwinism its peculiar character and importance. It is that Darwin rejects all teleology, or the doctrine of final causes. He denies de-

8. Hodge, *What Is Darwinism?*, 48–49.

sign in any of the organisms in the vegetable or animal world. He teaches that the eye was formed without any purpose of producing an organ of vision.[9]

The distinctive doctrine of Darwin centered on a belief that species owed their existence, not to the original purposes of a designer, but to the random consequences of time and chance. This doctrine, Hodge observed, could not be made hospitable to Christianity—or to any form of theism. Indeed, it was an intruder most deadly and dangerous. Darwin's challenge to biblical authority encompassed several broad themes. Obviously, if God's existence came into question, being preempted by materialism, then deity could not have produced a written record, infallible or otherwise. Worse yet, if God had not produced the Bible, then the ancients did so, making the written record of Scripture nothing more than the product of ancient historians far less informed than the enlightened thinkers of the nineteenth-century. Of course, this meant that Scripture possessed no authority at all. This sort of inevitable logical inference emerging from Darwin's materialism deeply troubled Hodge.

In light of such an aggressive competitor, Hodge sought to disprove Darwinian theory entirely. While Hodge considered theistic evolution tolerable (though unbiblical), he found Darwinian evolution as thoroughly intolerable. He recognized a growing chasm between men of science and of religion against which he chaffed. He stated:

> Religious men admit all the facts connected with our solar system; all the facts of geology, and of comparative anatomy, and of biology. Ought not this to satisfy scientific men? Must we also admit their explanations and inferences? If we admit that the human embryo passes through various phases, must we admit that man was once a fish, then a bird, then a dog, then an ape, and finally what he now is?[10]

Hodge believed that the scientific community had grown increasingly antagonistic to religion, demanding adherence not only to the facts of science but to the scientific explanations of those facts. Darwin only exacerbated the enmity. Hodge illustrated this growing antagonism toward religion generally and Christianity specifically, asserting that the intellectual respectability afforded to Darwinian theory had little to do with scientific evidence. Instead, he felt it represented a commitment to an emerging social philosophy which sought liberation from notions of divine

9. Ibid., 52.
10. Ibid., 132.

judgment and revealed religion, desiring freedom from any accountability to God. He noted in this regard:

> When the theory of evolution was propounded in 1844 in the "Vestiges of Creation," it was universally rejected; when proposed by Mr. Darwin, less than twenty years afterward, it was received with acclamation. Why is this? The facts are now what they were then . . . How then is it, that what was scientifically false in 1844 is scientifically true in 1864? . . . There is only one cause for the fact referred to, that we can think of. The "Vestiges of Creation" did not expressly or effectually exclude design. Darwin does. This is a reason assigned by the most zealous advocates of his theory for their adoption of it.[11]

In attempting to refute Darwin, Hodge noted, among other things, that the fixedness of species made macroevolution itself appear quite untenable. Since hybrids possessed no ability to procreate, it appeared that "God has fixed limits which cannot be passed."[12] Even such a naturalist as Thomas Huxley admitted that this represented an "insuperable objection" to Darwinian gradualism, Hodge noted.

The fossil record too argued against the gradual transmutation of life forms, indicating a sudden appearance of fully formed animals and plants rather than a slow development from one form to another. The fossil evidence suggested two irrefutable facts: (1) sudden appearance, and (2) stasis—or the lack of significant directional variation. Animals and plants appeared fully formed in the fossil record, exhibiting little significant alteration over time. These fossilized forms remained relatively unchanged in the fossil history from their initial appearances to their eventual extinction. Paleontology, therefore, Hodge argued, completely supported biblical teaching which stated that God created plants and animals with immediacy and after their own kind.

Furthermore, Hodge contended, Darwin was mute when it came to matters beyond the mere physicality of existing life forms. No mechanism was even suggested to explain the significant transition between dead and living matter. Darwin was left to assume both the existence of matter and the existence of life "in the form of one or more primordial germs."

Darwin said nothing, Hodge noted, in explaining consciousness or instinct among animals. How could instincts have originated? How could intermediate gradations account for them? Particularly troubling to

11. Ibid., 145–46.
12. Ibid., 158–59.

Darwin and fascinating to Hodge were cases of insect neuters—the sterile females within an insect community. Darwin noted that these insects often differed widely in both their instincts and their anatomic structures from males and fertile females. The problem for gradualism, of course, was that they could not propagate themselves, meaning that natural selection failed as an explanatory mechanism for their development.

Furthermore, Hodge observed, these neuters were not degenerations, but were frequently "larger and more robust than their associates."[13] Obviously, it is difficult to imagine how natural selection could be credited with such infertile consequences, since these insects did not reproduce and sterility could not be considered advantageous to the survivability of the neuters under any quantifiably reasonable measure.

Hodge attempted to refute Darwinism using empirical evidence and logical reasoning. He wanted to show the absurdity of Darwinism because Hodge viewed it as the equivalent to atheism. He reasoned:

> The conclusion of the whole matter is, that the denial of design in nature is virtually the denial of God. Mr. Darwin's theory does deny all design in nature, therefore, his theory is virtually atheistical . . . This is the vital point. The denial of final causes is the formative idea of Darwin's theory, and therefore no teleologist can be a Darwinian.[14]

Hodge had fully pledged himself to both a theistic worldview and to the inerrancy of the Scripture as the divinely inspired word of God. At one juncture he stated,

> It is conceded that a man may be an evolutionist and yet not be an atheist and may admit of design in nature. But we cannot see how the theory of evolution can be reconciled with the declarations of the Scriptures. Others may see it, and be able to reconcile their allegiance to science with their allegiance to the Bible.[15]

Though Hodge did not specifically articulate it, one might reasonably infer a lingering concluding thought in his mind—"but I cannot." If Scripture and science conflicted, Hodge would always render allegiance to the former. Hodge viewed evolution as potentially atheistic, Darwinism as absolutely atheistic, and both as inconsistent with the Scripture.[16]

13. Ibid., 36.
14. Ibid.,173, 175.
15. Ibid., 141.
16. Ibid., 22, 174–75. Hodge respected theistic evolutionists. These scholars retained

This was of the highest moment to Hodge, believing as he did that the Bible, in all its assertions, whether pertaining to matters of faith or fact—right down to the very words—was none other than the divinely inspired word of God. That Hodge defended both theism and inerrancy comes as little surprise, for conservatives had fought these same kinds of battles, though against different antagonists, throughout the century. Thus proponents of inerrancy of the original autographs continued to respond to their critics, maintaining that everything in Scripture was without error.

The High View and Its Competitors

In the face of these formidable challenges to biblical reliability, several theories of biblical authority and inspiration continued vying for ascendancy throughout the second half of the nineteenth-century. Three such theories continued to find support among Protestant theologians—the high view, a view which admitted the possibility of errors while denying that any such mistakes had as yet been discovered, and the partial theory. The high view continued to dominate, teaching that Scripture when properly interpreted was completely reliable in every detail.

Those endorsing this position believed that if a genuine error existed in the autographs, the entire biblical product became suspect. Divine inspiration guaranteed a composition completely reliable in every detail, no matter how exacting in nature. Opponents of this position contended that inerrancy represented an extremely hazardous opinion, placing the "Sacred Book, with all its contents, at the mercy of each of its minutest parts . . ."[17] Geologic science, Darwinian gradualism, and higher criticism of the Bible fueled these concerns mightily.

A second, related view, suggested that God never intended Scripture to teach scientific, historical, or geographic fact, but instead to instruct in moral and religious matters. Therefore, a mistake found in science, history, or geography would in no way detract from the authority of the Bible. But proponents maintained that no such discrepancies had been conclusively

---

a belief in God, while endorsing the mechanisms of progress associated with evolution theory—God began the process of creation, selecting evolution as the means to continue and complete it. While Hodge considered theism as immeasurably preferable to atheism, he nonetheless disparaged the willingness of theistic evolutionists to deviate from the biblical record of creation. Hodge considered theism without a dependable word from God as a shabby substitute for his position—inerrancy. This of course is not the least surprising, since Charles Hodge believed that everything addressed by the divine voice—whether pertaining to matters of faith or fact was necessarily perfect—down to the very words.

17. "Agreements and Differences Concerning the Bible," 80–81.

proved. Rather, they asserted that all apparent contradictions had been reasonably resolved, but admitted some minor inaccuracies might yet be uncovered. Advocates of this theory embraced scholarly criticism, believing that the integrity of Scripture would be unaffected by the existence of minor historical or scientific errors. Supporters of this view held Scripture in high esteem, considering its moral, ethical, and religious instruction inviolable.

A third theory admitted that "some imperfections amounting to erroneous statements in accounts of natural phenomena and in details of history and chronology existed."[18] While the Bible remained largely free from error, scholars endorsing this theory agreed, it was in no way inerrant. The mistakes found in the Bible came from either a poor memory on the part of the sacred penmen, ignorance, or misunderstanding. Deity did not see fit to enlighten the writer's minds in every profane or secondary matter. Proponents, consisting of an increasing number of Protestant theological liberals, emphasized the spiritual message of the Bible as the preeminent concern, relegating factual data to decidedly secondary importance.

This theory of inspiration represented a growing minority of biblical scholars devoted to higher criticism of Scripture and the secular sciences. Theologians representing this position believed that the best way to legitimize Christianity consisted in forthrightly admitting the failings of the Bible, and focusing on its spiritual message—just as Driver had done.[19] This outlook represented the perspective of the partial theorists, Protestant scholars deeply influenced by the emerging sciences who, as they saw it, sought to retain intellectual dignity for Christianity by admitting errors in Scripture which applied only to circumstantial concerns—i.e., to history and science.

18. Ibid., 81.

19. This editorial made several significant observations about all three theories of inspiration in common currency at this time. It stated, "The point to be made is that the second and third views as well as the first are plainly within the limits of evangelical faith . . . Both hold that the Bible records a divine revelation given to the world." The authors viewed the doctrine of inerrancy, with which theory they disagreed, as a legitimate evangelical position not as an innovative hybrid. Their principal concern over the inerrant position was that it kept the authority of Scripture in constant tension, demanding apologetic response every time a complaint was registered against its complete accuracy in every detail. The authors of the piece felt this was an unnecessary evil. Even so, they concurred that inerrancy was "the theory which is commonly supposed to be the most commendable . . ." Ibid., 82.

The High View Entrenched

Proponents of the high view offered firm resistance to what they rightly perceived as a growing erosion of confidence regarding the sacred text. Throughout the second half of the nineteenth-century advocates of inerrancy continued to staunchly defend it against the encroachments of the sciences and the higher critics. Benjamin Warfield, considered by many as the brightest luminary to come out of Princeton, remained doggedly committed to the inerrant stance throughout his career, arguing for its historicity. He called it the "church-doctrine of inspiration," asserting that from the ecclesiastical womb, the church had adhered to a belief in a totally errorless text of Scripture. The Early Church looked upon the Bible as an "oracular book—as the Word of God in such a sense that whatever it says God says . . ."[20]

Even contemporary critics of the high view doctrine admitted, Warfield argued, that from the earliest fathers of the church, verbal plenary inspiration and inerrancy had prevailed.[21] Warfield quoted from one noted higher critic, William Sanday, Professor of Exegesis at Exeter College, Oxford who, during the Bampton Lectures in 1893, conceded that the ancient church endorsed the verbal plenary doctrine of the Scriptures. Indeed, Sanday admitted the antiquity of this viewpoint, noting:

> Testimonies to the general doctrine of inspiration may be multiplied to almost any extent; but there are some which go further and point to an inspiration which might be described as 'verbal.' Nor does this idea come in tentatively and by degrees, but almost from the very first. Both Irenaeus and Tertullian regard inspiration as determining the choice of particular words and phrases. . . . Tertullian like Irenaeus, quite adopts the formula of St. Matthew and other New Testament writers as to the Spirit of God speaking 'through' the human author.[22]

Not only did Sanday buttress the historical argument set forth by Warfield on the ancient nature of verbal inspiration and the divine authorship of the Bible, but he further noted that the Early Church fathers believed that Scripture was without error. He stated:

> We cannot wonder if this high doctrine sometimes takes the form of asserting the absolute perfection and infallibility of the

20. Warfield, "Inspiration of the Bible," 616.

21. Ibid., 617.

22. Sanday, *Inspiration*, 34–35.

Scriptures. We saw that Irenaeus attributes to the Apostles 'perfect knowledge.' Elsewhere he is still more explicit, asserting that the Scriptures must needs be 'perfect, as having been spoken by the Word of God and His Spirit.'[23]

Warfield also cited support for the high view from the earliest creeds; among them the Apostles' Creed, the Augsburg Confession, and the Westminster Confession.[24] As many conservatives had done before him, Warfield, in discussing the basic assumptions behind the science of lower textual criticism argued that only the high view made sense of the industrious nature of their labors.[25]

Not only did the testimony of the early fathers, the affirmations of the church creeds, and the assumptions sustaining the work of lower textual scholars all endorse the inerrancy of the Bible in the original autographs, but the Scripture taught its own inspired status too, Warfield maintained. Inerrancy was the Bible doctrine before it was the Church doctrine. The writers of the New Testament and Jesus himself stood as unimpeachable witnesses to the doctrine of inerrancy. Warfield went on to contend that modern higher critics had largely concurred on that principle too, stating:

> it is not necessary to prove that the New Testament regards 'Scripture' as the . . . Word of God, in the highest and most rigid sense, to modern biblical scholarship. Among untrammeled students of the Bible, it is practically a matter of common consent that the writers of the New Testament books looked upon what they called "Scripture" as divinely safeguarded in even its verbal expression, and as divinely trustworthy in all its parts, in all its elements, and in all its affirmations of whatever kind. . . . This is common ground between believing and unbelieving students of the Bible, and needs, therefore, no new demonstration in the forum of scholarship.[26]

Having disavowed the need for evidence to support what was, Warfield argued, common knowledge, he nonetheless appealed specifically to the testimony of various higher critics to substantiate his assertion. Quoting a member of the "advanced school," Hermann Schultz, Warfield noted that Schultz admitted "The Book of the Law seemed already to the

23. Ibid., 36–37.

24. Warfield, "Inspiration of the Bible," 620–21.

25. Ibid., 619.

26. Ibid., 625.

latter poets of the Old Testament, the 'Word of God.' The post-canonical books of Israel regard the Law and the Prophets in this manner. And for the men of the New Testament, the Holy Scriptures of their people are already God's word in which God himself speaks."[27] The doctrine of the verbal inspiration and inerrancy of the canonical books dominated in the time of Christ, "and was shared by the New Testament men, and by Christ himself."[28] Thus Warfield applied many lines of argument to his case that inerrancy represented the church-doctrine from the very beginning.

Not only were prominent conservative scholars defending the strict view of inspiration, so too were front line pastors. One minister, E. F. Burr, contending for the inerrant view, wrote indignantly:

> Has it just been discovered that our copies of the Scriptures differ somewhat among themselves? Has it just come to the knowledge of the public that quotations from the Old Testament by the Master and his disciples were not always in the exact original words? Was it within the present century, or the last, that people found out that every sacred penmen has his peculiaries [sic] of both thought and expression? Certainly such facts were as well known to the fathers as they are to us. And yet those fathers stood up for the entire infallibility of the original Scriptures . . .[29]

The same prominent themes which appeared throughout the first six decades of the century in defense of inerrancy are common throughout this article. Burr asserted that the Bible was in fact errorless in everything to which it spoke—whether its voice addressed matters of doctrine or facts. This he contended, just as Warfield had done, echoed the nearly unanimous opinion of the Early Church. This ancestral conviction to inerrancy applied "no matter what the topic—whether fact or doctrine, whether sacred or secular, whether prose or poetry, whether chronology or history or science or religion . . ."[30]

27. Ibid., 626. Charles Briggs, a prominent partial theorist who takes center stage in the next chapter, buttresses the contention by Warfield that higher critics generally acknowledged the ancient character of inerrancy. In arguing that historical precedent is not always conclusive in determining doctrine, Briggs wrote, "Are we, then, to build the authority of the divine word on human authority? We do not give unquestioned allegiance to the early church in other matters of faith and practice, why should we grant them the last word as to the foundations of our faith? . . . No historical student can possibly accept any book as divinely inspired simply because the church of the first three centuries reached that conclusion." Briggs, "Whither," 81.

28. Ibid.

29. Burr, "Infallible Scripture," 121.

30. Ibid., 127.

Secular knowledge, the author asserted, far from damaging the testimony of the Bible, rather endorsed it. He stated, "That minute accuracy in even the most assailed parts of the Scriptures, to which it testifies, in regard to all the numerous points of the past which modern researchers have thus far been able to uncover, is sufficient warrant for assuming their accuracy at all other points."[31] Not only did the ancient church and modern scientific discoveries attest to inerrancy of the autographs, but Burr, as all conservatives before him, argued that the Bible taught its own inspired status.[32]

Furthermore, arguing that the Bible only spoke with inspired authority to "essential" things, as the liberals asserted, contradicted the entire lower critical endeavor, bent as it was on ascertaining the original readings of the text. What contribution did such an enterprise make, the author queried, if exactness of expression did not matter? Yet, the presumption of scholars committed to such a critical science hinged on the inestimable value of determining the precise language of the originals. Burr noted, "The whole effort of textual critics is to find out what the autographs were. This is considered immensely important, the great *desideratum*, deserving of almost unlimited pains."[33] A partial theory of inspiration made such zeal unnecessary, disparaging the toil of countless scholars and totally contradicting the basic assumptions under which they worked.

Burr also outlined the dangers associated with the lower theories of inspiration. If only the "main" things constituted the divine message, how could one determine the inspired from the uninspired parts? What criteria applied? Surely, the Bible offered no assistance in sifting through such a question. If human reason was the lone answer, how would differences of opinion be resolved? The author lamented, ". . . it is no easy matter to decide where 'main things end, and secondary or subordinate things begin. They shade away into each other as day does into night. Different men would draw the dividing line very differently."[34] The result of such a doctrine, he argued, would be uncertainty, endless disputes, and constant schism.

Just as conservative scholars in the 1850s had anticipated objections to the inerrancy of the autographs doctrine, so did Burr. What is the

31. Ibid., 129.
32. Ibid., 129–30.
33. Ibid., 134.
34. Ibid., 132–33.

use of such a doctrine if no original manuscripts remained extant? Burr responded:

> It is the use of having a perfectly solid foundation for a great edifice; of having a perfectly pure fountain to supply the successive reservoirs and pipes of a great city; of having a perfect standard of weights or measures to which to refer for verification. . . . It is the use of having a Bible mainly secure from error, instead of a Bible mainly open to error. . . . If only the copies are liable to error, then we have to discount from the infallibility of the book only at the points where the copies so differ among themselves as to make it hard to choose between them; but if the original Scriptures were themselves liable to error . . . the greater part of the Bible passes under a cloud. This, then, seems the proper doctrine. The original Scriptures, as they came fresh from the hands of the sacred penmen, were infallible in all their statements of whatever sort.[35]

Burr contended, as did virtually all conservatives, that inerrancy of the original autographs represented the ancient church doctrine, the biblical doctrine, and the only reliable doctrine, being absolutely essential to sustain biblical authority. Any other theory made the entire Bible debatable grounds, creating quicksand where once stood a firm foundation.

This kind of conservative clarion call replicated the defense tactics marshaled throughout the first six decades of the century. Another scholar, seminary professor Frederick Gardiner of the Berkeley divinity school in Connecticut, after admitting that copyist errors existed in the present text of Scripture, went on to argue for an inerrant original composition. Sounding very much like William Lee some twenty-five years earlier; he sought to demonstrate the perfect harmony of the teachings of Scripture against alleged inconsistencies and errors of fact. He noted, "As a single instance, in archaeology, ancient writers say that the vine was unknown in Egypt, and yet Moses mentions it; Egyptian hieroglyphics have been read, and it is found that Moses was right."[36] He contended that conservatives had so thoroughly answered the critical charges of internal inconsistencies that such assaults had generally fallen into disuse.

The maelstrom over the Mosaic cosmogony would no more taint Scripture than had the Copernican revolution hundreds of years earlier, the author asserted. Arguing, as his fellow conservatives had all along, that the language of sense rather than that of science had to be employed in order to communicate with the primitive audience to whom the initial

35. Ibid., 139.
36. Gardiner, "'Errors' of the Scriptures," 501.

message went. He continued to maintain the complete accuracy of the Genesis account when properly interpreted. He stated:

> The general order of creation is given with entire accuracy—first chaos, then light, then a fluid mass, then a separation of the dry land from the waters, then life beginning in its lowest vegetative forms and advancing through aquatic animal life to terrestrial, and all finally culminating in the appearance of man. . . . In this teaching there is no evidence of the error of imperfect knowledge, but only of an adaptation to the exigencies under which the revelation must be made. It leads men at once to the great features of the truth; it leads them to the exact detail, as far as they were capable of being led at the time; its apparent error is simply from its generality and brevity. To have been more precisely accurate . . . would have required a prolixity unsuited to the occasion.[37]

That the writers of Scripture spoke in an accommodating language in no way impugned their inspired message or its accuracy.[38] By necessity they addressed their hearers in the parlance of the times in an effort to communicate with, not confound, their listeners.

Sounding precisely like earlier high view advocates, Gardiner harmonized allegedly conflicting biblical statements, offering plausible explanations for the alleged discrepancies.[39] Gardiner concluded by insisting that

37. Ibid., 506–7.

38. Indeed, from the very first the Reformers realized that God had revealed his message by means of accommodating language. However, this divine condescension did not diminish the truthfulness or reliability of the Scripture. God communicated with human beings in the Bible, they assumed, as a parent might communicate honest and accurate information with a child using age appropriate language and imagery. In the eighteenth-century some critics, like Johann Semler, argued that *accommodatio* also implied the presence of erroneous statements as part of the revelation. Richard Muller rightly points out that such a view "has no relation either to the position of the Reformers or to that of the Protestant scholastics, either Lutheran or Reformed." Muller, *Dictionary of Latin and Greek Theological Terms*, 19.

39. In exactly the same manner as antebellum conservatives, this author suggested various remedies to harmonize apparent contradictions in the biblical text. The gospel account of the healing of Bartimaeus is a case in point. ". . . both Matthew and Mark expressly say that the event occurred when they had departed from Jericho, while Luke is equally definite in saying that it was when Jesus was drawing near to the city. . . . But it is altogether likely that our Lord on this journey spent several days at Jericho, and that, as was his custom at Jerusalem, and as is still the common custom in visiting Eastern cities, he slept in the country, and came daily into the city. This supposition, which is not only possible, but in itself probable, removes the whole difficulty. Matthew and Mark speak of the miracle as wrought when he had gone out from the city; Luke, more particularly, as exactly as he was entering it again on his morning return . . . An intelligent exegesis, seeking harmony,

other than errors of transcription, the Bible remained a completely perfect and reliable composition. He asserted that the sacred penmen, "touching upon every subject that came in their way—historical, ethnological, archaeological, scientific, and moral,—have been preserved from error."[40] Warfield, Burr, and Gardiner are illustrative of the kinds of arguments made in support of the high view by many leading conservative voices throughout the last decades of the nineteenth-century.

The Rise of Theological Liberalism

It is widely acknowledged that late eighteenth-century German liberal thought greatly influenced nineteenth-century American Protestantism.[41] Higher textual criticism and romanticism combined to alter the direction of biblical study, theological inquiry, and religious faith in Germany, eventually filtering into America.[42] The eighteenth-century German theo-

---

will always find it without strain." And again the author explained the alleged errors made by Stephen in Acts, "A more serious difficulty is found a little farther on, where he states (ver. 16) that the twelve patriarchs were buried 'in the sepulchre that *Abraham* bought for a sum of money from the sons Emmor.' Now, we know that Abraham bought a cave for a sepulchre at Mamre, but Joseph and his brethren were not buried there; we know, also, that Jacob bought a piece of land of the sons of Hamor near Shechem, and Joseph was buried there. Is it possible that Stephen in the haste of his utterance, mixed the two facts, and attributed to Abraham the purchase which belonged to Jacob? We think not; because in all probability, Abraham was the original purchaser of the same land afterwards purchased by Jacob, and this fact was known to Stephen. The evidence is as follows: The land about Shechem was already occupied (Gen. xii. 6, 7) when Abraham built an altar there. There were but three ways in which he could have done this: he must either have built it on the Shechemites' land, by their sufferance—an unlikely procedure for Abraham, and one giving no security for the sacredness of the altar; or he must have taken it by violence, which is improbable in the extreme; or, finally, he must have purchased it, which it reasonable to suppose he did. A century or more later Jacob came to the same place, and also wished to build an altar, presumably on the site of his grandfather's. But the land being occupied, this field would not have been left so long unoccupied, and Jacob doubtless found it in someone's possession. If he would reclaim it, it must either be by his sword, or by a fresh purchase. No one familiar with Jacob's character can doubt his choice, and his purchase is recorded." The extent to which advocates of the high view guarded the integrity of the biblical record attests to their persistence in asserting that Scripture was inerrant in every detail. Gardiner, "'Errors' of the Scriptures," 514–17.

40. Ibid., 533.

41. Indeed, William Hutchison called the great German theologian Frederich Schleiermacher, whom we shall consider presently, the "father of modern Protestant theology." Hutchison, *Modernist Impulse*, 7.

42. Of course the history of biblical higher criticism is complex and somewhat convoluted. Early modern fathers of higher biblical criticism include Baruch Spinoza, whose philosophical ideas significantly influenced Schleiermacher, Schelling, and Hegel. In his

logian, Gotthold Lessing (1729–81), one of the fathers of higher textual criticism, argued that Christianity "precedes the New Testament and is greater than the documents that represent it," maintaining that a critical assessment of existing errors in the text in no way compromised the value of Christian faith.[43]

Lessing, distinguishing between the religious feelings incited by the biblical books and the form of the books themselves, helped propel a movement that would eventually exalt emotions above reason and feelings over objective truth. He did not believe that the documents of Scripture possessed an errorless quality. Nor did he consider that problematic, for the Spirit applied each book's unique message to individual seekers.[44]

Gottfried Herder (1744–1803), another German critic of the eighteenth-century, moving in the same general direction as Lessing, argued that true religion involved more than knowledge or adherence to certain doctrines. Rather, in its essence Christianity revolved around an inner voice or conviction—an awareness of the presence of God in the heart of man. This transcendental notion would prove most appealing in America a century later.[45]

Both these scholars are indicative of a general drift in the late eighteenth-century away from German rationalism towards romanticism, placing an emphasis on feelings and imagination and a unity between the human and divine. This tendency deemphasized detached "facts" or the

---

Tractatus Theologico-politicus published in 1670, Spinoza challenged the Mosaic authorship of the Pentateuch, arguing that Ezra or some other late scribe produced the work. Another Dutchman, Jean Leclerc (1657–1763), expressly denied the Mosaic authorship of the Pentateuch, attributing the historical portions to King Josiah. The Frenchmen, Jean Astruc (1684–1766), appears to have been the first critic to suggest the use of different documents in order to compile the Pentateuch. He based his view on the various usages of the names for God—Elohim and Jehovah. This idea was greatly popularized and refined by the great German orientalist Johann Eichhorn who divided Genesis between the "Jehovist" and "Elohist" sources. Thus criticisms of the traditional views of biblical authorship and inspiration appear quite early. Nonetheless, the influx of romanticism combined with an increasingly ardent bent for criticism certainly influenced theological inquiry in Germany in the eighteenth-century, reaching America in full vigor in the next century. Cross, *Oxford Dictionary of the Christian Church*, 1300, 807, 100, 449.

43. Cross, *Theology of Schleiermacher*, 92.

44. Ibid., 93.

45. Transcendentalist or romantic Unitarianism insisted upon the immanence of God in both nature and in humanity. Unitarian theologians often used the term immanence to mean the indwelling presence of deity in humanity. Thinkers like Henry David Thoreau and Ralph Waldo Emerson are indicative of this viewpoint. The liberal theologian, Horace Bushnell, also stressed "God's indwelling [humanity] and humanity's direct intuitive access to the divine." Hutchison, *Modernist Impulse*, 19, 24, 44.

objective truths of Scripture and the documents in which they were expressed in favor of personal experience and communion with God.

In many respects Protestantism represented a revolt against the authority of the Church, asserting the right of Christians to think independently. Once Catholicism had been displaced as the unquestioned authority among Christians, a power vacuum developed that both Scripture and human reason sought to fill. The traditional Protestant paradigm, influenced by rationalism, sought to discover the facts of Scripture, aligning them in such a way as to create a compendium of doctrinal tenets demanding adherence; Christianity, therefore, centered on what one believed.

The scientific model, including careful observation of facts and induction, had generally prevailed in the post-Reformation period. While rationalism emphasized the intellect, romanticism exalted human imagination, passion and feelings. It was a mood or a tendency rather than an organized system, and it manifested itself in a variety of ways—including art, literature, and theological speculation.[46]

Perhaps no single thinker bore more of the responsibility for the tendencies associated with nineteenth-century American Protestant liberalism than did Frederick Schleiermacher. The son of a Reformed army chaplain, Schleiermacher was ordained to the ministry in 1794. Following his ordination, he received an appointment to preach at Berlin. It was at Berlin that he came into close contact with Frederick Schlegel and the teachings of Romanticism. Schleiermacher's written works exalted the place of experience in religion. Indeed, one might argue that for Schleiermacher religion was experience, a feeling of absolute dependence upon God and union with the divine.[47] Dogma, within such a model, necessarily played a decidedly secondary role.

Scripture generated religious feelings, serving as a tool plied by the Spirit to incite a conscious sense of the divine presence. The Bible, however, did not teach timeless eternal truth according to Schleiermacher. As a matter of fact, Schleiermacher seemed to indicate that truth was transient, fitted uniquely for every age. He noted:

> And when Holy Scripture is described as 'sufficient' in this regard, what is meant is that through our use of Scripture the Holy Spirit can lead us into all truth . . . Thus it is as representing each individual's personal understanding of Scripture that, in the measure of his command of thought and speech, his true expressions of Christian

46. Cross, *Oxford Dictionary of the Christian Church*, 1197.

47. Cross, *Theology of Schleiermacher*, 107–8.

piety take shape. And the interpretation of Christian faith which validates itself in each age as having been evoked by Scripture is the development, suited to that moment . . . and constitutes the common Christian orthodoxy for that time and place.[48]

He argued that the Bible was a living document employed constantly by the Holy Spirit, revealing new truths commensurate with the spirit of each successive age. The faith, therefore, was not "once delivered to the saints." Rather, the Spirit continued to deliver it, communing with and communicating new insights to Christians across time. Because Schleiermacher viewed religion as an immediate, personal, experience with the divine, he felt that the post-Reformation doctrine of inerrancy of the autographs, emphasizing the eternal truthfulness of the text, had violated the true essence of Protestantism.[49] He stated:

> If we consider the inspiration of Scripture . . . as a special portion of the official life of the Apostles which in general was guided by inspiration, we shall hardly need to raise all those difficult questions about the extent of inspiration which so long have been answered solely in a manner that removed the whole subject from the domain of experiential insight. Nothing but an utterly dead scholasticism could try to draw lines of demarcation anywhere on the pathway lying between the first impulse to write and the actu-

---

48. Macintosh and Stewart, *Frederick Schleiermacher*, 2:606.

49. Indeed, this same experiential paradigm is evident among others who challenged the doctrine of inerrancy, among them Samuel Coleridge. In his classic work *Confessions of an Inquiring Spirit*, Coleridge repeatedly asserted that the verbal plenary doctrine erred by making Scripture an objective statement of truth while deemphasizing the aspect of personal encounter with the Spirit through the text. He wrote, "With such purposes, with such feelings, have I perused the books of the Old and New Testaments . . . and need I say that I have met everywhere more or less copious sources of truth, and power, and purifying impulses;-that I have found words for my inmost thoughts, songs for my joy, utterances for my hidden griefs, and pleadings for my shame and weaknesses. In short whatever *finds* me, bears witness that it has proceeded from a Holy Spirit . . ." Coleridge, *Confessions of an Inquiring Spirit*, 42. He further asserted, in harmony with Schleiermacher, "Does not the universally admitted canon—. . . lead to the same practical conclusion . . . namely, that *it is the Spirit of the Bible, and not the detached words and sentences, that is infallible and absolute.* Coleridge, *Confessions*, 81. Interestingly, in all of this, Coleridge acknowledged that the doctrine of inerrancy was in fact the prevailing Protestant viewpoint on biblical authority in his day. He candidly stated that, "notwithstanding the repugnancy of the doctrine, in its unqualified sense, to Scripture, Reason, and Common Sense. . . . I must still avow my belief that . . . it *is* the Doctrine which the generality of our popular divines receive as orthodox. . . ." Coleridge, *Confessions*, 55.

ally written word, or wish to represent the written word in its bare externality as a special product of inspiration.[50]

In other words, those who emphasized the externals—the grammatical/historical meaning of Scripture—had at best missed the Bible's true intention and at worst had violated its real message. They had intellectualized the word, muting the clandestine communion desired by the hidden Spirit behind the word. Thus, Schleiermacher relegated objective doctrinal truth to a rather peripheral level, exalting the religious affections as primary.

Neither did Schleiermacher believe that the Bible taught its own inspired status, asserting that even if it did, only a precious few scholars could ever be certain of it.[51] He noted, "But even now, and even supposing that the inspiration of the New Testament Scriptures can be proved from these Scriptures themselves, this would nevertheless presuppose a very perfect understanding of these Scriptures."[52] Dogma, therefore, was of little importance to Schleiermacher, since religion, at its apex, produced "a sensation of union with the infinite."[53]

A number of important concepts associated with Schleiermacher's view of biblical authority influenced nineteenth-century Protestant liberalism. First, the verbal inerrancy of the text made little sense and was of even less concern to him, for the Spirit enlivened the meaning of the text in personal encounters. The voice of God was not confined to one oracular book from which to teach eternal principles. For the same reason, errors in matters pertaining to history, geography, and science presented no problem to him at all. The Bible and its author cared little for such mundane affairs; these circumstantial matters could not mute nor mitigate the voice of God to the individual worshipper who experienced the divine voice in the solitude of his own soul. Hence, the Bible conveyed solely a spiritual and contemporary message.

Second, Scripture never claimed the status of infallibility thrust upon it by the conservatives, urged Schleiermacher. Such a notion suggested a unique and timeless quality of truth for the text of Scripture. But, according to Schleiermacher, the Bible conveyed a spiritual message delivered to each individual privately in an experience of union with the divine.

50. Macintosh and Stewart, *Frederick Schleiermacher,* 2:599–600.
51. Ibid., 1:76.
52. Ibid.
53. Cross, *Oxford Dictionary of the Christian Church,* 1243.

Hence, Christianity consisted in not so much what one believed, but what one experienced.

Theological liberalism in America owed a great debt to thinkers like Lessing, Herder, and Schleiermacher. These German scholars created the theological network out of which the liberal Protestant impulse emerged. These same themes: an acceptance of errors of fact in Scripture, the claim that such errors were irrelevant, an emphasis on the spiritual message of the Bible, a rejection that Scripture taught its own inerrant status, a denial of the verbal inspiration of the text—all these assertions found expression in the writings of American Protestant liberals of the nineteenth-century.[54]

George Ladd, Congregational minister and professor at Yale College, typified the emerging liberal paradigm. He produced two weighty volumes on the inspiration and authority of the Scriptures published in 1883—spanning nearly fifteen hundred pages between them. In this work, Ladd repeatedly challenged the high view and its attempts to harmonize the biblical record, arguing that such exacting accord remained hopelessly elusive. Ladd, like many American liberals, blended rationalism, romanticism, and higher criticism, maintaining that human reason played the leading role for ascertaining the actual word of God from the biblical text.

Ladd anticipated three classes of readership who would likely engage his work: those who endorsed the inerrant view (which he considered the prevailing though flagging position), those who considered Scripture as a mere human composition, and those ready to embrace a new doctrine of Scripture—one which abandoned the minute details, focusing on the spiritual message of the Bible. Even in his denunciation of the high view, Ladd, as most liberals of his day, ceded the historical high ground to the inerrant view. He consistently referred to inerrancy as the traditional, post-Reformation opinion, stating:

54. As Hutchison observes, "Historians of religion have usually located the first stirrings of the so-called New Theology, or late nineteenth-century surge of liberal thought, in the New England Congregationalism of the years after 1875." Horace Bushnell, the theologian and Hartford preacher, serves as one of the fathers of late nineteenth-century New England liberal thought along with William Ellery Channing. Bushnell argued that Scripture had to harmonize with scientific truth in order to retain its legitimacy regardless of the concessions needed to do so—even if that meant accepting the presence of errors in the text. In his 1868 article "Science and Religion" he wrote, "Religion must consent to be configured to all true points of science . . . it [the Bible] must be converted to the world. And it can never stop being thus converted, till science stops making discovery. It must seek to put itself in harmony with every sort of truth else it cannot be true itself." Bushnell, "Science and Religion," 272–74. Bushnell often harmonized science and the Bible as liberals increasingly did—by spiritualizing Scripture in order to protect it from conflicting with prevailing secular ideas. Hutchison, *Modernist Impulse*, 48.

The only attempt which any large section of the Christian Church has ever made, rigidly to formulate the doctrine of Sacred Scripture, resulted in what we have called the post-Reformation dogma. This dogma was dominant in the Protestant, and especially in the Reformed churches, from about the year 1600 AD until the middle of the eighteenth-century. . . . The dogma with a sure instinct seemed to feel that its life in the future depended upon its ability to defend successfully the diplomatic infallibility of Sacred Scripture.[55]

Aligning with the third class of potential readers, Ladd expressed optimism about his position and its growing prowess. His goal, expressly stated in his introduction, amounted to a bloodless coup, amicably dethroning the high view position. He wrote:

There is yet another and third class of readers,—a class which I am glad to believe is rapidly coming to constitute the majority . . . Many of this class have already become convinced of the partial untenableness of the views which have been so largely current for the past two and a half centuries; but, as to precisely what views can be substituted for these untenable views, they are still in a position of doubting and waiting.[56]

Ladd offered an "enlightened" alternative to Christians who felt they could no longer accept the doctrine of inerrancy. They still believed in the major tenets of Christianity but not the doctrine of Scripture commonly asserted. In denouncing the verbal plenary doctrine, Ladd nonetheless frankly confessed that it had existed as the dominant theory of biblical authority in Protestantism for over two hundred years, before deteriorating in Europe at the hands of textual critics like Lessing and Herder. The erosion process spread far less rapidly in America, as Ladd's attempted overthrow in 1883 indicates.[57] Ladd argued that the "old orthodoxy," had outlived its usefulness, because otherwise "inspiration is . . . separated from its living and organic connection with revelation, and is conceived of something at-

---

55. Ladd, *Doctrine of Sacred Scripture*, 1:9.

56. Ibid., 1:viii.

57. Indeed, the 1880s represented a season of significant turbulence and challenge for the high view. Controversy stepped up its pace during this time, resulting in several clashes between conservative and liberal forces. The Presbyterian imbroglio created by the higher critical assertions of Rev. Charles Briggs is indicative of the general maelstrom of the times. The Briggs scenario is considered in detail in chapter four. Hutchison, *Modernist Impulse*, 77.

tached to a writing, rather than wrought out in a personality. It loses, then, its character of personal communion between two spirits . . ."[58]

Arguing in precisely the same terms as had Schleiermacher, Ladd contended that only that which spoke to the heart of an individual could lay claim to divine origin. Just as for Schleiermacher, inspiration, according to Ladd, did not apply strictly to the writings of the canonical books, rather he viewed it as a living dynamism, repeatedly occurring and reoccurring between the reader and the Spirit of God encountered in the text. In this way Ladd blended both rationalism and romanticism, while embracing the Germanic text critical theories.

The faculty of the conscience rather than the intellect became the medium through which God communicated with and had access to human beings. The duty of the Christian in every age remained constant, Ladd argued, to evaluate the Scripture in order to distinguish between the sacred and the profane. Assigning, in essence, three divisions to Scripture, Ladd believed that the words of Christ stood of highest authority, followed by the apostolic witnesses, due to the promise of Christ to guide them in their words. But Ladd considered the Old Testament generally non-binding and often irrelevant except for its important Messianic prophecies.[59]

Infallibility had to be rejected according to Ladd for the simple reason that the Scripture contained irreconcilable errors and mistakes. The conflicting witness of the gospel writers as to chronologies, names, numbers, and customs stood as hopelessly inconsistent, Ladd asserted. The Old Testament frequently endorsed immoralities and practices incompatible with the enlightened spirit of true New Testament Christianity. Prophecies often did not come true, indicating that the seers made mistakes in judgment and prediction. Ladd noted in this regard:

> We confess, therefore, the imperfection in form of Old-Testament prediction, and the failure of some of its more particular expectations . . . We also find certain mistakes as to alleged correspondences of form. We may ascribe the insight to inspiration, and the mistakes to rabbinical training and a lack of hermeneutical skill.[60]

Though mistakes regarding actual historical events commonly occurred, Ladd argued that the spiritual message of the prophets came to pass enigmatically. He stated, ". . . in brief, all the Old Testament predictions of Messianic salvation are, both as to substance and form of truth,

58. Ibid., 2:454.
59. Ibid., 2:578 and 1:444.
60. Ibid., 1:442, 445.

typically fulfilled in Jesus Christ."[61] Scripture proclaimed a spiritual message, according to Ladd, one deciphered spiritually with the assistance of higher text criticism.

Truth mixed with error best described the condition of the Bible—a condition which no amount of creativity or juggling of facts could ever harmonize, he argued. Trying to explain away all the various contradictions and discrepancies in the Bible, Ladd viewed as utter folly. It amounted to a juggler trying to keep a hundred balls airborne at once, being both impossible and ridiculous. He noted, "We cannot save the Bible as a whole to the satisfaction of human reason, when we have once committed its case to the infallibility of its separate parts."[62] Ladd believed, as did nearly all partial theorists, that their position alone represented the viable option, one which could rescue Christianity in an enlightened, scientific, text critical age. Adherence to inerrancy amounted to an assault on human reason and simply missed the point, they concluded.

Writing a year after the publication of Ladd's book, another partial theorist liberal, I. P. Warren, had much the same to declare about the Bible. The duty of the believer consisted in judiciously sifting out the divine from the common in the sacred text—and since the Bible contained much that was common it required diligent effort. He noted "That which is to be our guide . . . a clew [sic] of safety through all the intricacies involved in the connection between the divine and human in the Bible, is an enlightened and sanctified *common sense*.[63] Thus, man became the enlightened arbiter of the written word, judging the holy from the profane.

But did human beings possess the abilities necessary for such a sacred mission? Protestant liberals never doubted it. In explaining how to hear the voice of God in the Bible, the author asserted, "But it is man's prerogative and duty to discern his utterances, and to distinguish them from what are not his, and by his own nature as a moral being he is endowed with a capacity for doing so."[64] But what about the complaint that the partial theory reduced the Bible to the status of a sycophant, a slave subject to the subjective whims of each interpreter? The author addressed that concern too, writing:

> I am aware that it may be said that this is to make the word of God the subject of every man's caprice. That will have authority which

61. Ibid., 1:444.
62. Ibid., 2:685.
63. Warren, "Inspiration of the Old Testament," 323.
64. Ibid., 324.

he chooses to acknowledge. Any portion that he cannot reconcile with his own judgment he may set down as no part of God's utterance, and so escape its claims. But this is a perversion of our doctrine. . . . I did not say that human caprice was to be the judge, but common sense, *enlightened* and *honest.*[65]

Conservative scholars considered the distance between caprice and common sense dangerously narrow. Nevertheless, theories of inspiration that elevated the spiritual message of the Bible without getting bogged down in details pertaining to science and history increasingly gained currency as the century progressed. This of course, was precipitated by the text critical sciences, romanticism, advances in geology, and the looming shadow of Darwinian theory. Protestant liberals argued that in order for Scripture to retain authority, abandoning old notions of absolute perfection became essential. Since higher criticism, they believed, had revealed incontestable errors within some portions of Scripture, no enlightened modern could respect a doctrine that failed to frankly admit these mistakes, they argued. The best course of action included facing these contradictions squarely and refocusing on the "main" things. In this way, they assumed, Christianity would be protected and the Bible insulated from the assault of criticism, exerting no force against issues of the soul.

Theological conservatives mounted a cogent offensive against the liberals, arguing that they acted hastily in their rush to judgment, failing to extend the benefit of the doubt to the sacred writers. Ladd, they argued, did not offer the common courtesies afforded to all faithful historians regarding alleged errors and purported historical gaps. Ladd saw irreconcilable contradictions where they in fact did not exist. In responding to Ladd's charges, proponents of the high view employed the same tactics that typified their predecessors from the first half of the century. As one scholar, taking Ladd to task in a review, noted:

Dr. Ladd's principle of procedure seems to be, to affirm a positive and unexplainable discrepancy wherever one might by any possibility be supposed to exist; treating the Bible as if it had no positive claims upon our general confidence. The length to which Dr. Ladd goes, not only in suggesting, but in positively affirming, irreconcilable discrepancies in the Bible, has rarely, if ever, been surpassed.[66]

---

65. Ibid., 325.

66. "Dr Ladd on Alleged Discrepancies and Errors in the Bible," 389.

The reviewer argued that once a writer established his credibility and the "general correctness of their writings" had been determined, fairness demanded a sincere effort to search out a reasonable explanation to any alleged error. Ladd, his critic asserted, operated on the assumption that the sacred writers could not be trusted. Wherever any apparent contradiction occurred, Ladd presumed the worst—assuming the presence of a genuine error.

Internal discrepancies among the gospel witnesses proved the inerrancy doctrine both misguided and futile, Ladd argued. He stated, "But the Gospels contain also the complete refutation of the post-Reformation dogma of infallibility as applied to the historical contents of the Bible."[67] Ladd went on to state that those who expected Scripture to speak with an authoritative voice to matters of history had completely misunderstood its intended message.[68]

Ladd argued, the reviewer observed, that a clear contradiction occurred in the gospels regarding the discussion of Christ and the rich man. In Matt 19:17, Jesus, in replying to the wealthy youth said, "Why asketh thou me concerning that which is good? One there is who is good." While in Mark and Luke's account Christ's reply reads, "Why callest thou me good? None is good save one, *even* God." Professor Ladd asserted that both forms of the reply could not be accurate—not in an exacting nature. The reviewer responded to this charge, stating:

> In order to warrant Professor Ladd's unqualified assertion, he must assume, without evidence, and against all probability, that the evangelists give a complete account of all the conversation that took place between Christ and the rich young man; whereas, no one with any reasonable amount of historic imagination would ever think of assuming that the evangelists purport to give an exhaustive account of the transactions and conversations of their Lord. Any one. . . can easily see that in an interview of half an hour, or ten minutes even, there would be superabundant opportunity for the points of attack and defense to shift not only once . . . but a score of times . . . [69]

---

67. Ladd, *Doctrine of Scripture*, 1:400. It should be stored in memory, however, that Ladd repeatedly acknowledged the traditional nature of the inerrancy doctrine. He considered it an important product of the Reformation Era. This admission, by one of inerrancy's chief antagonists, will become crucial in assessing the claims of innovation made by a different higher critic, as will be explored in the following chapter.

68. Ibid.

69. "Dr. Ladd and Errors," 390.

Ladd found another gospel discrepancy regarding the Sermon on the Mount, saying that the accounts found in Matt 5–7 and Luke 6:17–49 are so "essentially two different, and in some respects discrepant, accounts that no harmony is possible. We are thus, at best, left in difficulties both critical and dogmatic."[70] Mathew states that Jesus went up into a mountain to teach, while Luke records that the instruction occurred on a level place. However, as the reviewer noted, there are in fact many level plains on mountains, amounting to no real contradiction at all. Furthermore, Luke provides a condensed version and Matthew an expanded account, all to be expected among historians with their own unique purposes for writing.

Summary

And so the parrying continued with both the critical and conservative advocates doing their utmost to vanquish the other side. While frequently suffering flesh wounds, both sides managed to guard their vital organs from the slashing indictments of their opponents. The conservatives responded to late nineteenth-century criticism in exactly the same manner as did their predecessors. They consistently sought to deflect charges of inconsistencies, errors, and discrepancies by suggesting what they considered reasonable explanations for them. They refused to acknowledge the presence of even one genuine flaw of any sort in the autographs. Critics, on the other hand, continued to disparage the historical, scientific, and factual accuracy of the Bible, contending that Scripture spoke with authority only to matters of faith.

Several interesting observations emerge. First, all sides in the debate, up until the 1890s, readily acknowledged that the inerrancy doctrine represented the "old orthodoxy," the "post-Reformation dogma," and the "traditional view" of biblical inspiration—which in fact prevailed within Protestantism for at least two hundred years. Ladd acknowledged that it had maintained hegemony for at least that long following Luther's Protestant rebellion.

Second, those endorsing the higher critical approach made no attempt to cloak their theory in the garb of antiquity, freely admitting that their view represented an enlightened modernism. They gloried in this fact—something new and exciting had emerged which would draw the best young minds to the study of Scripture. One advocate of the higher critical approach spoke of the advances in biblical studies based on text critical theories as the dawn of a new day, stating, "The Bible has been

---

70. Ladd, *Doctrine of Scripture*, 1:402.

born again. . . . Indeed, the closing half of this century is witnessing as immense an upheaval and advance in theology as recent years have seen in geology, and largely from the same cause."[71]

Third, though late nineteenth-century higher critics felt that the inerrancy position placed Christianity in jeopardy and constant tension, they nowhere denounced it as a doctrine out of concert with mainline evangelical thought or faith. Several positions regarding biblical authority belonged within the mainstream they argued, and inerrancy was among them. Critics of inerrancy in the late nineteenth-century typically argued for the need to replace the traditional view with a new model of biblical authority. Echoing George Ladd, another higher critical scholar noted:

> The theory which is slowly giving way, in the face of incontestable facts, a theory which became definite not long after the Reformation, and in consequence of the enthronement of the Bible in place of the church, is the theory that the Bible is true in every part, that its every statement may be relied on as correct. The inerrancy and complete infallibility of the Bible are maintained. . . . This is a fair account of the theory which has been commonly held.[72]

Fourth, conservative scholars in the second half of the century adopt-ed the exact same defense mechanisms as did their antebellum theological brethren. Burr, Gardiner, Hodge, Warfield and most other conservatives offered the identical arguments in support of their position as did Leonard Woods, Archibald Alexander, Robert Haldane, Lemuel Moss, Alvah Hovey, William Lee, Eleazar Lord, Enoch Pond, Charles Hodge, and a host of other prominent conservatives in the first half. The chain of scholarship endorsing the inerrancy of the original autographs remained unbroken throughout the century. These scholars served as key spokesmen and leaders among the Presbyterians, Congregationalists, Methodists, and Baptists.

High view advocates persistently sought to harmonize every alleged contradiction and error in the Bible, insisting that everything to which the divine voice spoke was necessarily perfect, whether pertaining to mat-ters of faith or fact. The primary evidence for their theory remained the Bible. Every conservative appealed to Scripture as their primary source of evidence, while also leaning on such ancillary support as the ancient and Reformation church, Creeds, the basic assumptions empowering lower textual criticism and the like. The similarities throughout the century are striking and fully sustained. Furthermore, if they could not account for ev-

71. "The conflict between Religion and Science," 451.
72. "Editorial," 301.

ery discrepancy, conservatives, from the opening moments of the century, appealed to the original autographs as a potential solution to the most vexing biblical conundrums. Transcriber errors accounted for some, if not all, of the most stubborn charges of the higher critics, they asserted.

The sciences; geology, Darwinism, and higher textual criticism placed tremendous pressure upon the theological elite throughout the last decades of the nineteenth-century. Some responded by altering the traditional view, exclusively emphasizing the spiritual message of Scripture. Well-intentioned, they believed such a shift would preserve the intellectual integrity of revealed religion in an increasingly scientific age.

However, the intrusion from secular fields failed to dissuade conservative scholars from endorsing inerrancy. Instead, scientific and higher textual encroachments incited a fervent rebuttal from high view advocates. Appealing to Scripture, history, and logic, they marshaled a staunch defense of inerrancy, just as their antebellum peers had done before them. They would not compromise, arguing that Scripture, in the original autographs and rightly interpreted, remained the final arbiter of truth—a truth to which all challengers must yield. That inerrancy retained its ascendancy even until the close of the century is illustrated by one of the most celebrated of all ecclesiastical trials in America—the case of Professor Charles Briggs of Union Seminary.

4

The Case of Professor Charles A. Briggs

Inerrancy Affirmed

CHARLES Augustus Briggs, ordained Presbyterian minister, Hebrew scholar, seminary professor, and committed proponent of the partial theory of inspiration, found himself squarely in the center of what was, arguably, the most spectacular and significant heresy trial in nineteenth-century America. The events leading up to and surrounding the trial greatly illuminate the debates on biblical authority in America, demonstrating both the tenacity of the high view and its broad endorsement.[1]

Briggs had challenged the strict theory of inspiration throughout the 1880s in his published works. However, it was his Inaugural Address at Union Seminary on the occasion of his induction into their newly endowed Edward Robinson Professorship of Biblical Theology which provoked a formal investigation into his doctrinal convictions, resulting in a heresy trial. This chapter investigates the events leading up to formal charges against Briggs and the trial itself, including the findings of both the Presbytery of New York and the General Assembly at Washington, D. C., where over five-hundred and fifty Presbyterian ministers and elders convened to judge the soundness of Professor Briggs's doctrine. This examination palpably reveals the vital place that the inerrancy of the original autograph doctrine occupied within the Presbyterian Church of the United States.

The Prelude

A prolific author, Briggs published a number of significant books during the 1880s, including *Biblical Study* in 1883. In this work he clearly took aim at what he considered an erroneous and dangerous doctrine—the iner-

1. Excerpts of this chapter appear in Satta, "Case of Professor Charles A. Briggs," 69–90.

rancy of the autographs of Scripture. Briggs, in his introduction, ascribed such a misguided faith to Scholasticism and Rationalism.[2] The doctrine resulted from an irrational deduction which neither Scripture nor history sustained, Briggs argued.

Like all partial theorists, Briggs sought to prove that errors did in fact exist throughout Scripture, but that these mistakes of "inadvertence" constituted no significant problem at all. Rather, their existence lent authenticity to the Bible, something that an errorless composition would entirely lack. Not only did he challenge inerrancy, but he specifically targeted Princeton theologians, including A. A. Hodge and B. B. Warfield along with the Seminary's President, Francis Patton. Briggs stated:

> That there are errors in the present text of our Bible and inconsistencies, it seems to us vain to deny. . . . There are chronological, geographical, and other circumstantial inconsistencies and errors which we should not hesitate to acknowledge. . . . It is claimed by some divines that the *inerrancy* of Scripture is essential to the inspiration of the Scriptures, and that 'a proved error in Scripture contradicts not only our doctrine, but the Scriptures claims, and therefore its inspiration in making those claims' . . . . These representations of the doctrine of inspiration have no support in the symbols of faith of the Reformation, or in the Westminster Confession, or in the Scriptures. [3]

The disdain with which Briggs held the original autograph idea could hardly be concealed. He considered it a position lacking both biblical and historical support.[4] Dangerous and noxious, inerrancy, Briggs argued, by its very nature generated malaise and constant tension among students of the Bible, making Scripture never stronger than its weakest link. He noted in this regard, "We hold that it is an unsafe position to assume, that we must first prove the credibility, inerrancy, and infallibility of a book ere we accept its authority."[5] As most partial theorists, Briggs considered inerrancy an unnecessary burden and a threat to enlightened Christianity. In another work Briggs spoke of inerrancy as "an awful doctrine to teach in

---

2. Briggs, *Biblical Study*, viii, ix.

3. Ibid., 240–41. Briggs is quoting F. L. Patton, the President at Princeton—Hodge and Warfield made use of this same logical syllogism in their article "Inspiration" published in 1881.

4. Ibid., 241.

5. Ibid., 243.

our days when biblical criticism has the field," and argued that "no more dangerous doctrine has ever come from the pen of men."[6]

Conservative scholars, very much aware of their formidable opponent, sparred with Briggs throughout the eighties. C. Frederick Wright, a professor at Oberlin Theological Seminary, took Briggs to task for his censure of the Princetonians and their commitment to inerrancy of the autographs. Wright argued that the proponents of the inerrant position did in fact have biblical and historical evidence to buttress and sustain their beliefs. Defending the Princetonians, Wright stated:

> For they and the scholars agreeing with them are emboldened to take this position both by the claims of the sacred writers themselves and by the futility of all the efforts during these eighteen hundred years to convict the Scriptures of any error. So universally have these efforts at criticism failed, that the presumption is exceedingly strong that the original writers did not make any mistake.[7]

Wright went on to challenge Briggs's assertion that the Scriptures contained errors, even in the original composition. If only by *a priori* reasoning could one assume the errorless quality of the autographs as Briggs argued, Wright asserted that the same assumption necessarily applied in presuming them error filled. Yet, Wright contended that the evidence sustained a presumption of perfection rather than perversion.

For instance, Briggs stated that an error must have occurred in the original text of Matt 27:9 in which Matthew attributes a certain quotation to Jeremiah when in fact, as per Scripture, Zechariah uttered the words. But, Wright asked, which seemed the most likely blunder, that the gospel writer erred or that a later copyist did so? Wright answered his own query, noting, "For our part we have no hesitation in saying that the error is most likely to have originated in the transcripts."[8] So long as the debate remained at the elite levels of scholarly inquiry a certain professional decorum presided over the debates. However, once the position of Briggs spilled over into the general public, ecclesiastical fireworks ensued. The inaugural address made by Briggs at Union Seminary provided the occasion of such a flash of light and smoke, where rather than confining his thoughts to writing, Briggs verbalized them.

The Board of Union Seminary, by unanimous vote, had selected Professor Charles Briggs to occupy the newly endowed chair known as

6. Briggs, *Whither*, 64, 73.

7. Wright, "Dr. Briggs 'Wither,'" 138.

8. Ibid., 140.

the Edward Robinson Professorship of Biblical Theology, established by means of a generous bequest by Charles Butler, the President of the Board of Directors at the school.[9] The auspicious inaugural festivities, set for Tuesday evening 20 January 1891, did not portend the ominous events to follow. It was upon this night that Briggs delivered his inaugural message, a speech which incited such heated reverberations as would conclude in a heresy trial and conviction, defrocking Briggs and banishing him from the ordained Presbyterian ministry.

In the days following his speech, Briggs would be charged with holding several heretical doctrines. The one that concerns this investigation pertains to his view of Scripture. In his address Briggs spoke plainly to important issues regarding the Bible and what he considered impediments keeping many people away from its study. He specifically discussed the doctrine of verbal inspiration, naming it as one of the "barriers" to biblical study. An inspiration of the original manuscripts which extended to the very words and phrases of the text, Briggs considered absurd. He noted,

> It is claimed for these originals by these modern dogmaticians that they are verbally inspired. No such claim is found in the Bible itself or in any of the creeds of Christendom. And yet it has been urged by the common opinion of modern evangelicalism that there can be no inspiration without *verbal inspiration.*[10]

Briggs also forthrightly addressed the doctrine of inerrancy of the autographs, dismissing it as a "ghost of modern evangelicalism."[11] Such a fiction, Briggs asserted, possessed no biblical, historical, or creedal support. The errors of the text revealed by modern criticism made such a doctrine patently ridiculous. Briggs stated:

> It is not a pleasant task to point out errors in the sacred Scriptures. Nevertheless, Historical Criticism finds them, and we must meet the issue whether they destroy the authority of the Bible or not. . . . I shall venture to affirm that, so far as I can see, there are errors in the Scriptures which no one has been able to explain away; and the theory that they were not in the original text is sheer assumption. . . .[12]

9. Briggs, *Authority of the Holy Scripture*, 9.

10. Ibid., 31.

11. Ibid., 35.

12. Ibid.

The presence of errors in the Bible should neither surprise nor frighten students of Scripture, Briggs asserted. After all, it was written by fallible human beings, though to be sure under the general supervision of deity so that its spiritual message retained full integrity. Briggs noted in this regard, "for these errors are all in the circumstantials and not in the essentials; they are in the human setting, not in the precious jewel itself. . . ."[13]

Moreover, Briggs littered his address with allusions to the callow nature of the inerrancy of the autograph doctrine, calling it "modern" and "recent," and without historical precedent. The doctrine of verbal inspiration, he contended, was the product of "modern dogmaticians" and the theory of inerrancy of the autographs had been taught only in "recent years."[14] He sought to emphatically condemn such notions, writing, "But on what authority do these men drive men from the Bible by this theory of inerrancy? The Bible nowhere makes this claim. The creeds of the church nowhere sanction it."[15]

Regarding Scripture, Briggs argued that errors existed in not only the present copies, but also most certainly in the original manuscripts. Inspiration extended only to the thoughts—to the spiritual message of the Bible, excluding matters of history, geography, science, and other factual data. The doctrine of inerrancy of the autographs and verbal inspiration represented merely the jangling of evangelical moderns, lacking precedent in either Scripture or history. Higher criticism, according to Briggs, had revealed its nascent origins.

In all this Briggs served as the archetype of the modern critical theory opposing the Princetonians and modern fundamentalism. Indeed, in his self-defense during trial, Briggs argued in the precise language employed by recent critics of inerrancy, revealing in the process the roots, not of fundamentalism, but of the modern critique of it. Of course, it is noteworthy that Briggs was overwhelmingly condemned for his views on the doctrine of Scripture, judged as a heretic as we shall see presently. The reason for this is that many of the mainline denominations in the nineteenth-century were in fact "fundamental" well before the fundamentalists.

The Uproar

Swift and sweeping best describes the reaction to Briggs's address, with many presbyteries registering concern and complaints over the doctrines

13. Ibid.
14. Ibid., 31, 35.
15. Ibid., 35.

espoused by him. Such a clamor arose that the New York Presbytery formed a Prosecuting Committee to investigate the transcript of the speech and offer recommendations on any further course of action. On 13 April 1891 the Presbytery of New York appointed an Investigative Committee consisting of Rev. George Birch, Rev. Joseph Lampe, Rev. Robert Sample, and Ruling Elders John Stevenson, and John McCook to examine the Briggs address.

They took their work seriously, studying the document over the next several weeks. On 11 May they reported their findings, recommending that "the Presbytery enter at once upon the judicial investigation of the case."[16] Their recommendation received approval by the Presbytery, who requested that the Committee continue prosecuting the case according to the rules of the Presbyterian Book of Discipline. Significantly the Presbyterian Church of the United States became the prosecutor. This fact would become vital since the New York Presbytery inclined toward leniency much more readily than would the General Assembly.

On 5 October 1891 the Prosecuting Committee presented specific charges of heresy against Briggs, delivering a citation to Briggs informing him of the specific allegations. They also requested that he appear before the New York Presbytery to respond to the charges. The Committee had leveled eight broad claims of heresy against Briggs, including issues pertaining to the place of reason, the role of the church, the authenticity of Scripture, the authorship of Isaiah, and the inerrancy of Scripture.[17]

Briggs appeared before the Presbytery on 4 November to respond. He affirmed his loyalty to the Scriptures as the word of God and to the Westminster Standards, arguing that some of his inaugural statements had been taken out of context by critics. Before the Prosecuting Committee had time to state its case against Briggs, a motion was made by Rev. Henry Van Dyke calling for a dismissal of the case against Briggs. Of course, Briggs had many friends and associates among the ministers, being a member of the New York Presbytery himself. The Presbytery agreed with the motion, dismissing the case in the following resolution:

> Resolved, that the Presbytery of New York, having listened to the paper of the Rev. Charles A. Briggs, D. D., in the case of the Presbyterian Church in the United States of America against him as to the sufficiency of the charges and specifications in form and legal effect; and without approving of the positions stated in his

16. McCook, *Briggs Heresy Case*, 13.

17. *Defense of Professor Briggs before the Presbytery of New York*, v, vi.

Inaugural Address, at the same time desiring earnestly the peace and quiet of the Church, and in view of the declarations made by Dr. Briggs touching his loyalty to the Holy Scriptures and the Westminster Standards, and of his disclaimers of interpretations put on some of his words, deems it best to dismiss the case, and hereby does so dismiss it.[18]

The Prosecuting Committee screamed foul, demanding that the case receive a more thorough treatment by the Presbytery. The desire for "peace and quiet" did not eclipse the need for an honest examination of potentially destructive heresy, they argued. They produced an appeal upon six general complaints including twenty-five specific procedural errors. The Presbytery, they alleged, did not try the case based on the evidence of the charges—but had simply taken Briggs at his word—amounting to no real trial at all.

They delivered the appeal to the State Clerk of the New York Presbytery who then sent it, along with other notes and documents regarding the trial, to the Judicial Committee of the General Assembly at Portland, Oregon, for further review. The General Assembly, the Supreme Court of the Presbyterian Church, considered the merits of the appeal. They invited both the Appellant and the Appellee to appear before them on 28 May 1892 to argue reasons for and against the appeal. Following the debate, the General Assembly voted on the twenty-five specifications of error submitted by the Prosecuting Committee, upholding the validity of each charge. The vote of the Commissioners was not close, with four-hundred and thirty one voting to sustain the appeal and eighty seven against.[19] The Assembly sent a terse note of response back to the New York Presbytery which read:

> It is now, May 30, 1892, ordered, that the judgment of the Presbytery of New York, entered November 4, 1891, dismissing the case of the Presbyterian Church in the United States of America against the Rev. Charles A. Briggs, D. D., be, and the same is hereby, reversed. And the case is remanded to the Presbytery of New York for a new trial . . .[20]

The Presbytery of New York received this mandate through the State Clerk of the Presbytery at its monthly meeting held on 13 June 1892. The Assembly had judged that the one day hearing of Briggs had been deficient and far from thorough. The New York Presbytery would not make the

18. McCook, *Briggs Heresy Case*, 16.
19. Ibid., 18.
20. Ibid., 19.

same mistake twice. While they deemed the sweltering months of summer a poor time to hold an ecclesiastical trial, they promised to redress the issue in a detailed and exacting manner come fall.

Indeed, they did devote significant attention to the matter, beginning their investigation afresh on 9 November 1892. At each session well over one-hundred ordained ministers and Ruling Elders convened at Scotch Church promptly at two o'clock to hear statements for the day. Including the initial meeting, the Presbytery met twenty times from their first gathering to their concluding session. Meeting mostly between Thanksgiving and Christmas, they convened on 28 and 29 November, and on 1, 5, 6, 7, 8, 13, 14, 15, 19, 20, 21, 22, 28, 29, and 30 December.

Briggs offered an extensive explanation and defense for the positions under consideration at trial. Charge number three pertained to the inerrancy of the Holy Scripture. The charge against Briggs read as follows:

> The Presbyterian Church in the United States of America charges the Rev. Charles A. Briggs, D. D., being a Minister of the said Church and a member of the Presbytery of New York, with teaching that errors may have existed in the original text of the Holy Scripture, as it came from its authors, which is contrary to the essential doctrine taught in the Holy Scriptures and in the Standards of the said Church, that the Holy Scripture is the Word of God written, immediately inspired, and the rule of faith and practice.[21]

The official position of the Presbyterian Church held that no errors of any kind existed in the original autographs penned by the sacred writers. They believed that such a position did in fact have biblical and historical support. The heresy of which they accused Briggs involved teaching against inerrancy.

The Defense of Briggs

The manner in which the defendant sought to justify his position is enlightening. He asserted his orthodox belief in the Holy Scripture as the Word of God, that it was in fact "immediately inspired," and that Scripture constituted the rule of faith and practice.[22] In this affirmation Briggs felt that he fit comfortably into the Reformation legacy. However, he disavowed any belief in inerrancy of the original autographs.

---

21. *Defense of Professor Charles Briggs before the Presbytery of New York*, 84.
22. Ibid., 88.

Briggs argued in his own defense from a number of different angles. Regarding the presence of errors in the autographs, Briggs candidly admitted that he did in fact believe "that errors may have existed in the original text of Scripture, as it came from the hands of the authors."[23] However, he did not consider such a position as a departure from traditional orthodoxy. He challenged the dogma that Scripture taught such a doctrine as inerrancy and denied vigorously that the Standards did so. Briggs stated:

> But we are bound as Presbyterians only to the essential and necessary articles of the Westminster Confession. We are not bound to unnecessary and unessential statements of the confession. Still less are we bound to statements which are not in the Confession at all, but which are regarded as logical deductions from the Confession by a party in the Church.[24]

Briggs further argued that errors or mistakes in matters pertaining to history and science did not detract at all from the divine voice in matters of faith and practice. He claimed that "the only errors I have found or ever recognized in Holy Scripture have been beyond the range of faith and practice, and therefore do not impair the infallibility of Holy Scripture as a rule of faith and practice."[25] Briggs believed that one could endorse the declaration of the Standards that "Scripture is the Word of God written" without committing to inerrancy in every detail. The errors of the Bible, Briggs noted, were all in matters of "inadvertence" not of deceit or falsehood. The Bible, Briggs contended, did teach all that was necessary to salvation and godly living. In all these vital matters of faith the Scripture spoke perfect truth. However, Briggs felt that an artificial dogma had been added to the concept, including inerrancy in every detail. He noted that the Confession:

> . . . teaches that God 'committed wholly unto writing that knowledge of God and of his will which is necessary unto salvation.' This statement I sincerely adopt. But note what was committed 'wholly unto writing': 'the knowledge of God and of his will which is necessary unto salvation'—nothing more; not the knowledge of geography, not the knowledge of chronology, not the knowledge of correct citations, not exactness in names of persons, and things, unless you can prove that these are necessary to salvation.[26]

23. Ibid., 84.
24. Ibid., 87–88.
25. Ibid., 89.
26. Ibid., 93.

For partial theorists as Briggs, factual data represented matters of secondary, if not completely inconsequential, concerns. He felt that some scholars had made leaps in logic that neither Scripture nor the Confession warranted. Briggs subscribed to the Westminster Catechism that Holy Scripture "is the Word of God" and that "it contains the Word of God." For Briggs being "the Word of God" meant that Scripture contained the rule of faith and practice. That Scripture "contained the Word of God" implied that "this rule of faith and practice so fills and pervades and controls Holy Scripture as to make it to all intents and purposes the Word of God."[27] But Briggs challenged the implications made by the inerrantist party that these statements endorsed verbal inspiration and accuracy in every particular.

Briggs further argued his case from the Confessional statement on Scripture which declared its "immediately inspired" quality. Briggs quoted the Confession citing section eight, which reads, "The Old Testament in Hebrew and the New Testament in Greek, being immediately inspired by God and by his singular care and providence kept pure in all ages . . ."[28] Briggs connected the doctrine of immediate inspiration with the following phrase which declares its perpetual purity, arguing that as far as its intended purposes are concerned, the Bible is errorless.

He interpreted the adverb "immediately" not as relating to the original autographs as did the inerrantists, but as pertaining to the Greek and Hebrew copies. He asserted "the Confession does not say, 'having been immediately inspired by God,' referring to their origin in the past, but 'being immediately inspired by God,' alluding to their present condition."[29] In other words, Briggs believed that the Hebrew and Greek copies actually possessed within themselves the "divine grace of inspiration" as opposed to translations in which the inspiration was "mediately" from God through the "medium of the originals."[30] Therefore, the adverb "immediately," Briggs argued, did not support inerrancy for he felt it had nothing to do with the original autographs.

He sought to sustain this argument by stressing the doctrine of perpetual purity mentioned in the Confession. The Confession states that by the providence of God, the Greek and Hebrew manuscripts were kept pure through the ages. But Briggs noted that the copies in the original

27. Ibid., 95–96.
28. Ibid., 97.
29. Ibid., 97–98.
30. Ibid.

languages contained hundreds, even thousands, of minor variants between them. Their purity did not extend to matters of grammar or syntax, including the words or phrases of the text. How then could conservative scholars sustain their doctrine of verbal inspiration and inerrancy, since the purity of the text patently did not include such matters? In contrast, Briggs, affirming the confessional doctrine, argued that purity included all the purposes for which God delivered the Scripture, namely, for all issues of faith and practice. Briggs noted:

> Pure, yes, for its purpose of grace and salvation. Pure, yes, to determine infallibly controversies of religion. Pure, yes, to give the infallible rule of faith and practice and to determine every question of religion, doctrine, and morals. Pure, yes, so that these great purposes of the grace of God shall in no wise be contaminated, or colored, or warped, or changed in the slightest particular; but not pure in the sense that every sentence, word, and letter of our present Greek and Hebrew text is absolutely errorless and inerrant.[31]

Of course, Briggs begged the question by inserting "our *present* Greek and Hebrew text" since no theologian held to the error free quality of the present copies. The point of conflict reposed over one's position on the original manuscripts not the extant copies. Indeed, the original autograph issue represented the real concern. Nevertheless, Briggs concluded this phase of his defense arguing that errors enhance rather than detract from the force of the Bible. He asserted:

> Indeed, the study of the errors of the Holy Scripture is one of the strongest evidences of the credibility of the Scriptures. It shows clearly that the text has in all ages been kept pure for its purposes of grace and salvation. All the errors that have yet been discovered are but as moles on a beautiful face . . .[32]

And so Briggs vigorously maintained his orthodoxy as measured against the Bible and the Westminster Confession, asserting in the process that those espousing inerrancy represented the real heretics. He affirmed his belief in the Scripture as the Word of God, upheld the doctrine of "immediate inspiration," and agreed that the Bible constituted the only rule of faith and practice. Briggs, however, interpreted all of these positions in such a way as to not only avoid inerrancy but to condemn it.

31. Ibid., 99.
32. Ibid., 102.

On 9 January 1893 the Presbytery of New York made its final judgment in the Briggs case. A committee consisting of Rev. George Alexander,
Rev. Henry Van Dyke, and Elder Robert Jaffray expressed the findings of
the Presbytery in the following words:

> The case of the Presbyterian church in the United States of
> America against the Reverend Charles A. Briggs, D. D., having
> been dismissed by the Presbytery of New York on November 4th,
> 1891, was remanded by the General Assembly of 1892 to the
> same Presbytery, with instructions that 'it be brought to issue and
> tried on the merits thereof as speedily as possible.' In obedience
> to this mandate the Presbytery of New York has tried the case. It
> has listened to the evidence and argument of the Committee of
> Prosecution, acting in fidelity to the duty committed to them. It
> has heard the defense and evidence of the Rev. Charles A. Briggs,
> presented in accordance with the rights secured to every minister
> of the church. . . . Giving due consideration to the defendant's
> explanation of the language used in his Inaugural Address, accept-
> ing his frank and full disclaimer of the interpretation which has
> been put upon some of its phrases and illustrations, crediting his
> affirmations of loyalty to the Standards of the church and to the
> Holy Scriptures as the only infallible rule of faith and practice,
> the Presbytery does not find that he has transgressed the limits of
> liberty allowed under our Constitution to scholarship and opin-
> ion. Therefore, without expressing approval of the critical or theo-
> logical views embodied in the Inaugural Address or the manner
> in which they have been expressed and illustrated, the Presbytery
> pronounces the Rev. Charles A. Briggs, D. D., fully acquitted of
> the offences alleged against him . . . [33]

One might suppose that this decision would have resolved the matter. However, the vote of the New York Presbytery was close—an ominous
harbinger for Briggs. Regarding his doctrine of Scripture, charge number
three, sixty-one members of the Presbytery sustained the heresy charges
against Briggs while sixty-seven voted to remit them. Considering that
Briggs was a close friend and associate with many sitting in judgment
against him, the slim margin in his favor proved inauspicious.

Indeed, the Prosecuting Committee once again appealed the case,
this time requesting that the members of the General Assembly themselves hear it and judge the soundness of Briggs' position. Furthermore,
a close inspection of the judicatory statement of acquittal indicates that
the Presbytery sought to distance themselves from Briggs' position stating

---

33. McCook, *Briggs Heresy Case*, 20–21.

that dismissal came "without expressing approval of the critical or theological views embodied in the Inaugural Address." In essence, they gave
Briggs the right to his own scholarly opinions without endorsing them in
any way—a verdict which did not escape the attention of the Prosecuting
Committee members.

The request for appeal made by the Prosecuting Committee to the
General Assembly came affixed with a lengthy, detailed, and urgent message.
The Rev. Joseph Lampe addressed the Assembly with a series of complaints
about the proceedings in New York and the serious nature of the deviations
represented by the Briggs position. For one thing, he noted, though Briggs
declined to verify his testimony under oath, considering the request to do so
as preposterous, the Presbytery allowed him to function as both client and
counsel, taking his word as competent evidence.[34] He stated:

> The question to be determined is, whether or not the views of
> Dr. Briggs can be tolerated under the orthodox creed to which he
> subscribes; and to take his word for it is to evade the whole issue.
> . . . Dr. Briggs has, in fact, disclaimed nothing, but has distinctly
> reaffirmed all the views of his Inaugural Address of every kind.[35]

Lampe reminded the Assembly that Briggs was put on trial for his
critical views, none of which had been retracted. Why, he asked, did the
Presbytery acquit Briggs but at the same time distance themselves from his
position? He noted:

> The fact that they felt disinclined to acquit the defendant, with-
> out expressing a distinct disavowal of his critical and theological
> views for which he is on trial, leads to a very strong presumption
> that the decision is contrary to the evidence not only, but that
> those rendering the decision recognize the views of the defendant
> as conflicting with the Scripture and the Standards; for certainly,
> no body of Presbyterian ministers and elders need be at pains to
> disavow views which are in accord with the Bible and our Creed.
> The inferior judicatory, in this final judgment, has not given us
> either good Presbyterian law or doctrine.[36]

The Presbytery did not decide the case on its merits, Lampe argued, but
on the basis of the word of the accused. The finding of the New York
Presbytery was incongruous declared Lampe, acquitting the accused while
at the same time disapproving of "the very views which form the basis

34. Ibid., 274.
35. Ibid., 282.
36. Ibid., 281.

of the trial." The verdict, therefore, should be considered unjust, having no force to calm the disquietude which was evident throughout the Presbyterian Church, Lampe contended.[37] Elder Joseph McCook, in his much shorter request for appeal, noted the same incongruity, writing:

> In the final judgment of the Presbytery they declared that the said doctrines were not out of harmony with the Standards, although at the same time they affirmed that they did not intend to say that they approved of the defendant's views, which they had declared to be not unorthodox . . . the decision of the Presbytery of New York in this case is contradictory and illegal.[38]

In turning to the doctrine of inerrancy of Scripture, Lampe sternly censured the Briggs position as one out of concert with the Bible and the Standards. Briggs had admitted to teaching that errors are likely to be found in the original autographs, Lampe reminded the Assembly. This fact, he asserted, placed Briggs beyond orthodoxy, contradicting both the Scripture and the Standards. The Standards teach that the Scripture is the Word of God, and to assert that the original production could contain errors of any sort was to impugn God's character, Lampe urged.

Briggs had admitted his belief that certain errors of "inadvertence" permeated the Bible. And while the Standards do view some portions of Scripture as more vital than others, it nonetheless, teaches that all portions are "entirely truthful."[39] Professor Briggs contended that the Bible is literally filled with errors, containing lapses of memory and the like, and that these mistakes extend over large portions of both the Old and New Testaments. While the "precious jewel" was protected, great portions of the text evidently were not.

Inspiration, according to Briggs, did not prevent men from making the same kind of errors as any other human writer. Surely, Lampe complained, this does not represent the orthodox view, rather "it conflicts irreconcilably with the doctrine as formulated in the Standards."[40] The Standards affirm that the *writing* itself, not just the thoughts as Briggs believed, were inspired, resulting in an absolutely perfect record—entirely truthful in every respect.

Lampe challenged Briggs's interpretation of the adverb "immediately" in the Standards. Immediate inspiration did in fact refer to the original

37. Ibid., 285.
38. Ibid., 365.
39. Ibid., 301.
40. Ibid., 303.

writings, Lampe argued. The Confession declares that these originals came directly from God, possessing absolute accuracy and reliability in all they assert. The following phrase "and by his singular care kept pure in all ages" affirms their relative accuracy, asserting the general providential care of God in maintaining his word from any significant corruption. Immediate inspiration assured inerrancy—after all how could God, the author, make a mistake. Purity assured a clear, though less than perfect, word from God.[41] And though the copies had been mildly corrupted, the science of lower criticism could retrieve the actual wording of the original errorless text in most cases.

Not only did the Standards endorse inerrancy, Lampe argued, but so too did the Scripture itself. Lampe quoted 2 Tim 3:16 as evidence for the verbal inspiration and error free quality of the Bible. He also turned to 2 Pet 1:21 to buttress this contention, demonstrating that the Holy Spirit himself authored the text, proving that no error could possibly invade the original "God-breathed" manuscript. Lampe asserted that history firmly sustained the inerrant position and that it replicated the opinion of the New Testament Church as well as that of the great Reformers. While Briggs had appealed to history to support his doctrine, Lampe considered such a maneuver futile. All of the fathers and the Reformers belonged in the inerrant category, Lampe stated. He noted:

> It is preposterous at this late day to advance the claim that insisting on the truthfulness of the Bible is tantamount to setting up a new test of orthodoxy. The Church has never believed anything else. Especially is this true of the Presbyterian Church. It will not be possible to point to a single representative Presbyterian divine, from the Westminster period down, and especially among American Presbyterians, who has taught the doctrine of the errancy of Scripture. All sides, parties, and schools in our Church have been agreed in affirming the inerrancy of the Word of God. Green Alexander and Hodge cordially unite with Richards and Barnes in subscribing to the statement of Dr. Henry B. Smith that inspiration extends to both thoughts and words and gives us "truth without error" in the Bible. Our Church has always held that, when we have determined the exact historic-grammatical meaning of a statement in the Bible, we have then the absolute truthfulness of that statement certified to us by the Spirit of God.[42]

41. Ibid.
42. Ibid., 309.

Lampe and the Committee urgently requested one final appeal, to the Supreme Court of the Presbyterian Church in the United States—the General Assembly. Their appeal resonated with the Assembly, who ordered a new trial against Briggs set for May 1893 in Washington, D. C. Over five-hundred and fifty ordained Presbyterian ministers and elders convened in the nation's capital to consider the acceptability and orthodoxy of the doctrines espoused by Briggs.

In the early going, Briggs requested that the Assembly remand his case once again to New York, this time to be tried by the Synod (the ecclesiastical court directly above the Presbytery in rank). No doubt Briggs felt New York would provide friendlier confines than those of Washington. However, the Assembly rejected his request by an overwhelming margin—409–145. This time New York would not save Briggs.

Throughout his defense, Briggs, using many of the same arguments he had employed in New York, pleaded his own case.[43] Regarding the third charge, pertaining to the inerrancy of Scripture, Briggs continued to maintain his orthodoxy without consenting to the original autograph doctrine. Questions began the inquiry:

> *Question 2.* "Do you believe the Scriptures of the Old and New Testaments to be the only infallible rule of faith and practice?"
>
> Answer. "Yes."
>
> *Question 3.* "Would you accept the following as a satisfactory definition of inspiration: Inspiration is such a Divine direction as to secure an infallible record of God's revelations in respect to both faith and doctrine?"
>
> Answer. "Yes."
>
> *Question 4.* "Do you believe the Bible inerrant in all matters concerning faith and practice, and, in everything in which it is a revelation from God as a vehicle of Divine truth, and that there are no errors which disturb its infallibility in these matters or in its records of the historic events and institutions with which they are inseparably connected?"
>
> Answer: "Yes."

Though Briggs endorsed plenary inspiration and affirmed that Scripture is both "the Word of God" and "contains the Word of God" these orthodox agreements were not sufficient to render his doctrine of Scripture thoroughly orthodox, according to the Assembly.[44]

43. A. Stranger, *Trial of Dr. Briggs before the General Assembly*, 84–85.
44. Ibid.

The General Assembly accepted the definition of infallibility as set forth in the Webster's Dictionary, which defines infallible as "not fallible; not capable of erring; entirely exempt from liability to mistake; unerring, inerrable."[45] Measured against such a standard, Briggs's destiny looked foreboding indeed. Although one interested onlooker perceived an important misunderstanding between the Assembly and Briggs regarding the term "error" and "errors," the General Assembly viewed the defendant's readiness to assume mistakes in the original composition of Scripture as serious, troubling, and beyond the bounds of orthodoxy.[46]

The Prosecution argued that the Westminster Confession would not permit the presence of any errors in Holy Scripture since the Bible's entire perfection served as guarantor that it was in fact "the word of God." God, as the generative source of Scripture, could never fail to compose less than a completely inerrant record, whether the divine voice addressed sacred or mundane matters. Only by means of an error-free book could the Holy Spirit assure the believer of the "infallible truth and divine authority thereof."[47] A work containing mistakes and errors, even in secondary matters could not possess the quality of complete perfection, being marred in its assertions. Thus, the Holy Spirit could not attest to its infallible truth if in fact it erred.[48]

In the end, the alleged differences between "error" and "errors" amounted to but little. The Assembly was not interested in such fine points of discrimination. As they viewed things, Briggs believed that the sacred text, even in the original autographs, contained the same peccadilloes, foibles, and limitations as any other human composition—a position the vast majority of the Assembly considered intolerable.

On 1 June 1893 the General Assembly reached its verdict. They extended one last chance for Briggs to recant his views, including those on

45. Ibid., 101.

46. The anonymous writer using the pseudonym "A. Stranger" believed that Briggs used the term "errors" to mean something other than the Assembly. Briggs employed it to mean any false prescriptive teaching while the Assembly used it to mean any wrong statement of any kind—even if made in allegedly minor details. Briggs felt that inadvertent mistakes did not constitute an error. He affirmed the proposition that the Bible never taught error—but not that it contained no errors of any kind. For instance, in the secondary or circumstantial points of its address, the Scripture writers did occasionally make mistakes. This position proved fatal for Briggs in the trial. For the Assembly endorsed inerrancy—that the Scripture could not fail to be perfectly accurate when properly interpreted in every detail—whether pertaining to matters of faith or matters of fact—down to the very words.

47. Ibid., 98.

48. Ibid.

his doctrine of Scripture. He refused their courtesy, iterating his position and refusing to amend it in any way. As Rev. George Baker, Chairman of the Sub-Committee selected to compose the report against Briggs, noted on the morning of the final judgment:

> When the committee of fifteen convened this morning it was impressed with a sense of responsibility which seldom falls to the lot of men to bear. We all felt that the very first thing to do in all Christian love and courtesy, was to appoint a committee to call upon Dr. Briggs, and give him an opportunity to say whatever he might be pleased to say in view of the distressing circumstances. There was a prayer in our hearts that Dr. Briggs might be led of God to say something which would relieve the painful situation. I regret to say that our hope in this regard was disappointed. Our interview was frank, kind, and cordial to the last degree; but Dr. Briggs insisted strenuously, positively, and irrevocably upon everything that he had said in the defense which he made when brought to the bar of this court.[49]

Having failed to provoke any capitulation or compromise from Briggs, the Committee of fifteen drafted a report which the Assembly overwhelmingly approved. The final tally to sustain the appeal against the acquittal of Briggs stood at 383 to sustain and 116 not to sustain. Over seventy-five percent of the four hundred and ninety-nine votes cast by key leaders in the Presbyterian Church charged Briggs with holding heretical doctrines out of concert with orthodoxy. The final report, presented by the Rev. Thomas A. Hoyt, Chairman of the Committee on judgment, read in part:

> . . . on consideration whereof this judicatory finds that the final judgment of the Presbytery of New York is erroneous and should be and is hereby reversed; and this General Assembly, sitting as a judicatory in said case, coming now to enter judgment on said amended charges, one, two, three, five, six, and eight, finds the Appellee, the said Charles A. Briggs, has uttered, taught, and propagated views, doctrines, and teachings as set forth in said charges contrary to the essential doctrine of Holy Scripture and the Standards of said Presbyterian Church in the United States of America, and in violation of the ordination vow of said Appellee, which said erroneous teachings, views and doctrines strike at the vitals of religion and have been industriously spread; wherefore, this General Assembly of the Presbyterian Church in the United States of America, sitting as a judicatory in this case on appeal,

---

49. McCook, *Briggs Heresy Case*, 374.

does hereby suspend Charles A. Briggs, the said Appellee, from the office of a minister in the Presbyterian Church in the United States of America, until such time as he shall give satisfactory evidence of repentance to the General Assembly of the Presbyterian Church in the United States of America, for the violation by him of the said ordination vow as herein and heretofore found.[50]

Charles Briggs was found guilty of heresy and defrocked as an ordained minister in the Presbyterian Church, in part because of his refusal to endorse the doctrine of inerrancy of the autographs of Scripture. He failed to convince the Assembly of the soundness of his views or that inerrancy represented a callow doctrine out of step with traditional orthodoxy through the ages. Though Briggs affirmed the divine origin and perfect spiritual message of the Bible, being immediately inspired by God, and serving as the final arbiter in all matters of faith and practice, the Assembly judged his doctrine of Scripture too lax and in fact heretical.

The proceedings surrounding the trial and the court's final decision against Briggs serve to illustrate the intense commitment to the doctrine of inerrancy of the autographs common in the nineteenth-century. The Assembly concluded that to teach against it constituted an act of heresy, resulting, in this case, in the defrocking of Charles A. Briggs, D. D.

Implications of the Trial

This case is fascinating, not only in illustrating the tenacity of the high view as late as the close of the nineteenth-century, but also in serving as a portal into the rationale of the modern critical theory against inerrancy and those who endorse it. Charles Briggs appears to have served as the fulcrum for the development of a modern myth against the doctrine of inerrancy, Princeton, and American fundamentalism. Indeed, all the seeds of the modern critical theory are present in the unsuccessful defense of Professor Briggs. The means by which Briggs sought to fend off mounting criticism against his own views were themselves innovative. Other late-nineteenth century scholars, antagonistic towards inerrancy, challenged it in a very different manner than Briggs, by arguing for the need to replace the old orthodoxy with something new. The parallels between the modern critical view against inerrancy and the Briggs defense tactics are illuminating—and even startling.

The basic thesis of the modern critical school is that the inerrancy of the original autographs doctrine began with A. A. Hodge and B. B.

50. Ibid., 377.

Warfield in the late nineteenth-century as the pugilism of the critics drove Princeton scholars to fabricate this idea. It allegedly served as a duplicitous shield insulating the Bible from critical assault. But, as we have seen, the doctrine of the inerrancy of the original manuscripts existed in full vigor from the very beginning of the nineteenth-century to its close. It was entrenched in the writings of significant Protestant scholars on both sides of the Atlantic, including John Dick, Leonard Woods, Archibald Alexander, William Lee, Charles Hodge, Enoch Pond, Eleazar Lord, and others. So how did this misguided notion about inerrancy become the standard view among many modern scholars?

It seems likely that the answer to this enigma resides in the thrust and parry tactics of Briggs. In his defense before the New York Presbytery, Briggs sought to capture the historical high ground for the critical theorists, revising history in his favor. In defending his doctrine of Scripture, Briggs stated no less than ten times that inerrancy represented something new, modern, and callow. From the opening moments of his statement on Scripture, he sought to place the inerrant theory on defense, stating, "You may agree with a recent opinion that *'a proved error in Scripture contradicts not only our doctrine, but the Scripture's claims, and therefore its inspiration in making those claims.'*"[51] But Briggs certainly did not believe it. Briggs had quoted a statement made by Hodge and Warfield in their "infamous" article "Inspiration" published in 1881, making it appear that such a notion was recent—something innovative. This theme permeated his defense testimony. He asserted somewhat later that, "Modern biblical scholarship has forced the advocates of inerrancy . . . to rally about the modern dogma of the inerrancy of the original autographs."[52] Higher criticism precipitated the development of the original autograph dogma according to Briggs. This expresses the sentiments of modern critical scholarship exactly—criticism forced conservatives to concoct this new idea.

Briggs called inerrancy a product of "modern scholastics" who "by pure conjecture invent an inerrant original autograph theory."[53] Not only did the doctrine represent a callow position according to Briggs, but only very few theologians allegedly endorsed it. Briggs sought to marginalize inerrancy by asserting that only a small coterie of misguided theologues believed in it, writing, "There are a few professors in the Biblical department in American theological seminaries who hold to this modern dogma

---

51. *Defense of Briggs*, 85.
52. Ibid., 100.
53. Ibid., 100–101.

of inerrancy and in the interests of this dogma try to explain away the errors of Holy Scripture."[54] Relegating the inerrant position to a few professors in American seminaries—a mildly veiled censure of the Princetonians, Briggs sought to banish inerrancy to the religious periphery as a movement seriously out of concert with mainstream orthodoxy.

However, the Briggs challenge to the inerrancy doctrine as a modern artifice echoed in decidedly solitary tones. Even fellow critics of the doctrine of inerrancy betrayed the Briggs argument as hollow, lacking substance. George Ladd, the liberal Congregational clergyman and professor at Yale College, a stern critic of inerrancy, nonetheless asserted that it had prevailed as the post-Reformation dogma for well over two-hundred years.[55] Another vigorous opponent of inerrancy, William Sanday, Professor of Exegesis at Exeter College, Oxford, frankly confessed the ancient origin of inerrancy, arguing for its dominance throughout the New Testament period and beyond.[56] The historical legitimacy of inerrancy is a well attested fact, replete throughout the literature.

Is it possible that Briggs was simply uninformed regarding the historiography of the original autograph theory? Perhaps, though it seems more likely that Briggs functioned as a conscious reviser, hoping to persuade his judges that his view represented the truly historic position. He failed to convince them, for his arbiters nowhere concurred with his argument

---

54. Ibid., 105.

55. Ladd, as we have seen, frankly confessed the historical legitimacy of inerrancy, writing, "The only attempt which any large section of the Christian Church has ever made, rigidly to formulate the doctrine of sacred Scripture, resulted in what we have called the post-Reformation dogma. This dogma was dominant in the Protestant, and especially in the Reformed churches, from about the year 1600 AD until the middle of the eighteenth-century. . . . The dogma with a sure instinct seemed to feel that its life in the future depended upon its ability to defend successfully the diplomatic infallibility of Sacred Scripture" (Ladd, *Doctrine of Scripture*, 1:9). Ladd's candid admission stands in stark contrast to the assertion of innovation urged by Briggs in his defense.

56. Sanday conceded, "Testimonies to the general doctrine of inspiration may be multiplied to almost any extent; but there are some which go further and point to an inspiration which might be described as 'verbal.' Nor does this idea come in tentatively and by degrees, but almost from the very first. Both Irenaeus and Tertullian regard inspiration as determining the choice of particular words and phrases. . . . Tertullian like Irenaeus, quite adopts the formula of St. Matthew and other New Testament writers as to the Spirit of God speaking 'through' the human author. . . . We cannot wonder if this high doctrine sometimes takes the form of asserting the absolute perfection and infallibility of the Scriptures. We saw that Irenaeus attributes to the Apostles 'perfect' knowledge. Elsewhere he is still more explicit, asserting that the Scriptures must needs be 'perfect,' as having been spoken by the Word of God and His Spirit." Sanday, *Inspiration*, 34–37.

or the logic thereof. On the contrary, they sought to distance themselves from his defense tactics even in acquittal.

Briggs further criticized conservatives for insisting that the Bible taught its own inspired, inerrant status. He categorically denied such an idea asserting that "the Bible nowhere teaches it."[57] Briggs believed, as do modern critics of fundamentalism, that inerrancy resulted from defective logic, making deductions unwarranted by the biblical text. Rationalism is the common scapegoat blamed as the driving force behind the inerrant doctrine.[58]

However, the General Assembly knew better—they knew that conservative scholars throughout the century had constantly appealed to Scripture to support their theory—and indeed to construct it. High view advocates believed that the Bible did teach inerrancy, being the product of God's generative activity. As his voice, what could Scripture be other than a completely perfect composition? The product of serious, reflective analysis of the biblical record, inerrancy simply represented the position conservatives believed the Bible itself taught.

Briggs also stands as the paragon of the critical theory in that he placed Princeton squarely at the core of his criticism, implying that they taught and wrote as theological loners and isolated mavericks seriously out of step with traditional orthodoxy across time. He tried hard to marginalize them and the theory they represented. Yet, Princeton was anything but alone in its commitment to the inerrancy of the autographs as the decision of the ecclesiastical court clearly revealed. One is left with the queasy sense that Professor Briggs handled the evidence with something less than full candor. At least that was the decision of the General Assembly in 1893.

57. Briggs, *Authority of Scripture*, 35.

58. For instance, in his criticism of fundamentalism, James Barr contends that inerrancy is the product of rationalist philosophy. He states, "Nowhere is the rationalism of fundamentalist argument more apparent than in the doctrine of the inspiration and infallibility of the Bible itself. Though inspiration is mentioned in the Bible, nowhere does the Bible suggest that inspiration includes the package of implications taken as authoritative by fundamentalists; it nowhere says that this implies historical accuracy, it nowhere says anything about the original autographs. . . . The fundamentalist construction is not derived from what Scripture actually says but is derived rationally." Barr, *Authority of the Bible*, 70. Furthermore, George Marsden has observed that much of the work of Rogers and McKim was intended to portray the doctrine of the inerrancy of the original autographs as "the product of seventeenth-century Protestant scholasticism which was later falsely equated with classical orthodoxy by nineteenth-century Princeton Seminary theologians." Marsden, *Reforming Fundamentalism*, 285.

Conclusion

READING the treatment of biblical authority by historian Ernest Sandeen is like taking a trip in a time machine, transporting the reader back to the Briggs trial—revealing that the modern controversy over inerrancy is not really modern after all. Sandeen levels three complaints against A. A. Hodge and B. B. Warfield: that they taught (1) inspiration extended to the very words of the text, (2) inspiration extended only to the original autographs of Scripture, and (3) the Scriptures taught their own inerrancy.[1] These principles, he urged, just as Briggs had urged, were contrary to traditional orthodoxy, lacking precedent within the mainstream.

Sandeen even cites the twice-employed phrase used by Briggs in his defense in the same disparaging manner, asserting that inerrancy represented a misguided addendum to orthodoxy. He noted, "Warfield, in the strongest statement in the article, wrote: 'A proved error in Scripture contradicts not only our doctrine, but the Scripture's claims and, therefore, its inspiration in making those claims.'"[2]

The Briggs defense tactics parallel Sandeen's censure in hauntingly familiar tones. The culprit in both scenarios is the Princeton school, most especially A. A. Hodge and B. B. Warfield. These two scholars, the critics from both centuries assert, were responsible for fabricating a theological aberration—the doctrine of inerrancy of the autographs. Higher textual criticism serves both critical models as the catalyst which motivated them to do so. Sandeen states in this regard:

> Verbal and inerrant inspiration was claimed not for the Bible as we now find it, but for the books of the Bible as they came from the hands of the authors—the original autographs. This emphasis upon the original manuscripts is another example of the way in which the Princeton doctrine of the Scriptures was refined and tightened in the face of growing critical opposition . . . There can

1. Sandeen, *Roots,* 123, 125, 127–28.

2. Sandeen, *Roots,* 126. Sandeen is citing the article written by A. A. Hodge and B. B. Warfield, "Inspiration," *Presbyterian Review,* 238, 245.

be little doubt that biblical criticism was responsible for the hard-ening of the Princeton position.[3]

The "newly minted" original autograph doctrine, fresh off the presses at Princeton, represented an evasive maneuver to fend off charges of dis-crepancies and contradictions within Scripture and between the Bible and secular knowledge. Both Briggs and the modern critics have endeavored to relegate the Princetonians to the religious periphery, portraying them as out of accord with conventional thinking.[4] By depicting Princeton as the lone source of the autograph doctrine and marginalizing them, the natural corollary is to relegate their heirs, the fundamentalists, to the religious backwater too. The problem of course is that the critical theory is defec-tive, as the evidence reveals.

Both Briggs and the modern critical theorists believed that inerrancy lacked historical roots. Briggs argued that the great Reformers did not adhere to such a doctrine and Sandeen asserts the same thing, noting:

> This new emphasis [on the inerrancy of the original autographs] was introduced just at the time that the number of biblical errors or discrepancies turned up by the critics was growing too large to be ignored . . . The problems raised by biblical criticism demanded a new formulation of the doctrine of the Scriptures . . . The heart

---

3. Ibid., 127.

4. Sandeen is merely the most influential modern critic of the Princeton doctrine of inspiration, not the first. In his chapter on Charles Hodge in *The Lives of Eighteen from Princeton*, John Oliver Nelson suggested in 1946 that Hodge created a theological ab-erration—the doctrine of the inerrancy of the original autographs. In assessing Hodge's theology he wrote, "Nailed highest to the mast of his theological craft is the paramount claim—hailed by Yale in that period to be the one distinctive Princeton tenet—regarding the inspiration of the Bible. It is this: the original texts of Scripture, now lost, were letter-perfect as dictated by Deity, and any possible error has crept in since." Nelson, "Charles Hodge," 208–9. His comments about Yale's criticism are not documented—there is no footnote. Furthermore, Presbyterian historian Lefferts Loetscher also considered Hodge a theological maverick who broke ties with traditional orthodoxy by his doctrine of in-spiration. He suggests a theological conspiracy between Charles Hodge and his son, A. A. Hodge, in which they sought to insulate the Bible from criticism by appealing to the autographs. He wrote, Dr. Hodge intimated a distinction between the existing text of Scripture and the original text or autographs, which was to be much more emphasized by his son." Loetscher, *Broadening Church*, 24. However, the attempt to sequester Princeton as the genesis of the inerrancy doctrine is simply impossible to sustain when measured against the evidence. Such arguments seem myopic, focusing exclusively on Princeton while ignor-ing the widespread commitment to inerrancy among many other influential theologians from a variety of denominations.

of their position was the argument that God could not, would not, convey truth through an errant document.[5]

Yet, this was precisely the position endorsed by conservative scholars throughout the nineteenth-century. And while Briggs and contemporary critics have asserted that the original autograph doctrine represented a serious departure from the Reformation legacy, evidence from that period exists suggesting its presence long before the nineteenth-century in America. Since Briggs, a Presbyterian minister, appealed to the Reformation tradition to buttress his contention, it seems appropriate to briefly assess the doctrine of Scripture of one early Reformer who wrote an important book on the Reformed perspective on the Bible.

The doctrine of biblical authority endorsed by the Cambridge divine William Whitaker creates further difficulties for both Professor Briggs and the modern critical theorists.[6] Whitaker wrote extensively on the doctrine of Scripture. His book, *A Disputation on Holy Scripture,* was generally considered one of the seminal Protestant works on biblical authority. In this book Whitaker continually affirmed his belief in an errorless Bible. By contending that Scripture possessed such a status, Whitaker considered himself to be expounding the same doctrine as that held by Augustine. Whitaker stated:

> We cannot but wholly disapprove of the opinion of those, who think that the sacred writers have, in some places, fallen into mistakes. That some of the ancients were of this opinion appears from the testimony of Augustine, who maintains, in opposition to them, 'that the evangelists are free from all falsehood, both from that which proceeds from deliberate deceit, and that which is the result of forgetfulness.'[7]

Viewing himself in harmony with Augustine, Whitaker refused to allow for the possibility of any flaws in the Scripture. Only the sacred writers produced an errorless composition—they alone penned inspired writ. The Cambridge scholar possessed a comprehensive, clear position on inerrancy which he lucidly described while explaining the secondary role of the human agent:

5. Ibid., 129–30.

6. The Whitaker illustration also appears in Satta, "Fundamentalism and Inerrancy," 78–79.

7. Whitaker, *Disputation on Holy Scripture,* 36–37.

> They wrote as they were moved by the Holy Ghost, as Peter tells
> us, 2 Pet. i.21. And all Scripture is inspired of God, as Paul ex-
> pressly writes, 2 Tim iii.16. Whereas, therefore, no one may say
> that any infirmity could befall the Holy Spirit, it follows that the
> sacred writers could not be deceived, or err in any respect. Here,
> then, it becomes us to be so scrupulous as not to allow that any
> such slip can be found in Scripture.[8]

Whitaker believed that the Bible contained no errors, because deity had authored it. Since "no infirmity could befall the Holy Spirit," it
logically followed that the writers controlled by him in the transmission
process could not fail to articulate perfection. This is exactly the same position held by conservative scholars throughout the nineteenth-century. The
Holy Spirit authored the text, assuring a production free of errors in every
detail, whether pertaining to faith or facts—down to the very words.

Like the Princetonians, Whitaker's doctrine of biblical authority refused to admit even one error in the originals, believing that one such
mistake would controvert the authority of Scripture itself. In this respect
he sounds a great deal like Warfield whom both Briggs and Sandeen
criticized for writing "a proved error in Scripture contradicts not only our
doctrine, but the Scripture's claims, and therefore its inspiration in making
those claims." The Princeton theologians are charged with artifice, conjur-
ing up a callow doctrine which misrepresented traditional orthodoxy. The
evidence, however, refutes such a claim. Over two-hundred and fifty years
before Hodge and Warfield wrote their article, William Whitaker, taught
the same thing.

Perhaps Whitaker's dogmatism on this point emerges most clearly
in his confrontation with Melchior Canus. In an attempted solution to
an apparent biblical discrepancy, Canus submitted a remedy which suggested an error on the part of Stephen in the book of Acts. Whitaker's
view on an errorless text would permit no such conclusion. He opposed
Canus, arguing,

> Stephen therefore, could no more have mistaken than Luke, be-
> cause the Holy Ghost was the same in Luke and in Stephen, and
> had no less force in the one than in the other . . . Therefore, we
> must maintain in tact the authority of Scripture in such a sense as
> not to allow that anything is therein delivered otherwise than the
> most perfect truth required.[9]

8. Ibid., 38.
9. Ibid., 38.

Whitaker expected the Scripture to declare perfect truth, just as did nineteenth-century proponents of the high view of inspiration. Whitaker's doctrine of biblical authority was comprehensive and well-defined: (1) all Scripture is the product of the Holy Spirit; (2) Scripture contains no errors of any kind in anything it asserts; (3) to admit the presence of even one genuine error in the autographs was to impugn God's integrity, because he is the author. Whitaker endorsed biblical inerrancy—hundreds of years before Hodge and Warfield roamed the corridors at Princeton.

In the late nineteenth-century Professor Charles Briggs employed a strategy against inerrancy that failed. In it he sought to recast the doctrine as a recent innovation, a misguided addendum possessing neither biblical nor historical sanction. He argued that it represented the opinion of only a small group of isolated American theologians, most particularly those operating out of Princeton, and most especially A. A. Hodge and B. B. Warfield. Higher biblical criticism had compelled them to engage in a theological conspiracy in their quest to maintain biblical authority. Likely, Briggs was seeking to secure legitimacy for Christianity in the face of surging secular knowledge and an intensifying cross examination of Scripture by both secular and sacred critics. The General Assembly of the Presbyterian Church of the United States of America found his argument less than persuasive, because they knew that the preponderance of biblical and historical evidence weighed heavily against him.

Why the alleged facts offered by Briggs failed to resonate in 1893 but became common scholarly currency after 1970 is something of a mystery. However, one may speculate. Charles Hodge, in assessing the rapid intellectual respectability offered to Darwinian gradualism after other theories of evolution had been rejected, asserted, "When a drama is introduced in a theatre and universally condemned, and a little while afterward, with little change . . . it is received with rapturous applause, the natural conclusion is, that the change is in the audience and not in the drama."[10]

The theological scholar/leaders that heard and assessed the Briggs defense strategy did so with a keen awareness of nineteenth-century theological convictions regarding the Bible. They knew that the conservative voice had prevailed throughout most of the century, endorsing the high view of inspiration. However, after the theological controversies of the 1920s and 1930s had displaced the doctrine of inerrancy among many mainstream Protestants, some scholars may have simply assumed that it had lacked significant biblical, theological, and historical support. By

10. Hodge, *What is Darwinism*, 145.

1970 liberal scholars were more than ready to accept any plausible, if less than thorough, study explaining how inerrancy emerged as an aberrant doctrine out of concert with Protestant orthodoxy since the Reformation. The conclusion rather than the argument itself is what interested them most. The audience, not the facts, had changed.

A modern mythology rising from the ashes of the failed Briggs defense has relegated fundamentalism to the intellectual and religious periphery, marginalizing it in precisely the same manner as Briggs sought to marginalize Princeton. But the fundamentalists were not the innovators, they were the standard-bearers. They represented high view advocates from many mainline nineteenth-century Protestant denominations, including the Presbyterians, Baptists, Congregationalists, and Methodists, existing as part of a conservative theological legacy that pervaded mainline thinking for most of the nineteenth-century.

The roots of American fundamentalism are much deeper and wider than its critics concede.[11] One will not find them in the late nineteenth-

---

11. Indeed, scholars remained a bit nonplused as to the precise identity of the fundamentalists throughout much of the first half of the twentieth-century, emerging as they did from many denominational groups. While modern stereotypes often assume that Premillennialism represented a basic tenet, early fundamentalist writings seem to refute such an idea. Charles R. Erdman, while arguing for an imminent return of Christ, appears quite willing to embrace dissenters as part of the fundamentalist contingent, writing, "However great the divergence of views among students of prophecy may seem to be, and in spite of the many varieties of opinion among the representatives of the two schools which have been mentioned in passing [post-millennialism and pre-millennialism], the *points of agreement* are far *more important*. The main difference is to the order, rather than as to the reality of the events. The great body of believers are united in expecting both an age of glory and a personal return of Christ. As to many related events they differ; but as to the *one great precedent condition* of that coming age or that promised return of the Lord there is absolute harmony of conviction: *the Gospel must first be preached to all nations* (Matt 24:14). Erdman, "Coming of Christ," 4:312. Though liberty prevailed regarding eschatological convictions, an endorsement of the high view of Scripture represented a critical concern and foundational belief among the fundamentalists as James Gray, Dean of Moody Bible Institute, makes plain. Interestingly, Gray appealed to the findings of the General Assembly of 1893 for unimpeachable evidence for inerrancy, writing, "But we conclude with a kind of concrete testimony—that of the General Assembly of the Presbyterian Church of America, and of a date as recent as 1893. The writer is not a Presbyterian, and therefore with the better grace can ask his reader to consider the character and the intellect represented in such an Assembly. Here are some of our greatest merchants, our greatest jurists, our greatest educators, our greatest statesmen, as well as our greatest missionaries, evangelists, and theologians . . . For sobriety of thought, for depth as well as breadth of learning, for wealth of spiritual experience, for honesty of utterance, and virility of conviction, the General Assembly of the Presbyterian Church in America must command attention and respect throughout the world. And this is what it said on the subject we are now considering at its gathering in the city of Washington, the capital of

century as is often supposed. Nor is their heritage circumscribed solely by the Princeton scholars. Indeed, their roots are far deeper than the parameters of this study, confining itself as it does principally to the nineteenth-century. For as the curtain of the nineteenth-century opened, the doctrine of the inerrancy of the original autographs was already deeply engrained within the fabric of traditional Protestantism, indicating a lineage far more prominent and ancient than is commonly believed.

---

the nation, at the date named: 'THE BIBLE AS WE NOW HAVE IT, IN ITS VARIOUS TRANSLATIONS AND REVISIONS, WHEN FREED FROM ALL ERRORS AND MISTAKES OF TRANSLATORS, COPYISTS, AND PRINTERS, (IS) THE VERY WORD OF GOD, AND CONSEQUENTLY WHOLLY WITHOUT ERROR.'" Gray, "Inspiration of the Bible," 2:42–43. Inerrancy not eschatology was one of the key doctrines most vigorously endorsed by early fundamentalists. On this issue no latitude existed.

Appendix

Historiographical Postlude

"Inspiration"—A Closer Look

SINCE the critics argue that inerrancy was introduced by young Hodge and Warfield in their 1881 article "Inspiration," it is worth assessing their complaint specifically and directly. This postlude does just that, investigating their accusation more fully. As a lapidary examines a gem from many points of light, so the critical conspiracy theory must be evaluated from several angles.

Regarding the article published by Warfield and Hodge, several questions demand further examination. First, logically what value would a fabricated theory have had in the midst of the critical debates? Second, textually does their article "Inspiration" depend on the autograph argument—was it crucial to their defense of the Bible? Third, exegetically did such a "dodge" actually make the Bible impregnable to attack?

Logically, if the sacred writers themselves (the holy men, the apostles and prophets) wrote by divine inspiration at the precise moment of their composition (as many nineteenth-century scholars assumed), what other conclusion could one reach about the status of the original manuscripts? The first edition text had to be the inspired version because the Holy Spirit produced the document using the sacred writer as his amanuensis. What else other than the originals could be rightly defined as "God-breathed?"[1]

Copyists, whom no one considered inspired, simply sought to reproduce the original text. However, as the evidence makes plain, theologians had long realized that errors of the eye, ear, and hand produced unavoidable textual corruptions. Some scribes proved malicious in their textual emendations and others made well-intentioned but misinformed corrections to the text. This is precisely why lower textual critics had long employed their expertise in seeking to reconstruct the most likely render-

---

1. Satta, "Fundamentalism and Inerrancy," 66–81. The following section contains an excerpt from this article.

ing of a given passage by comparing the various readings among available copies. This procedure revealed the assumption of biblical scholars—that no text was perfect. Copies were not synonymous with inspired originals. To argue that they were confuses the doctrine of inspiration with that of preservation; an error which Sandeen apparently has stumbled into but of which no nineteenth-century theologian was guilty.

Furthermore, would such a novel ploy have really benefited the inerrant cause? In the midst of the raging debates over biblical authority and inspiration, is it likely that young Hodge and Warfield would have resorted to unheard of tactics to defend Scripture's integrity, knowing the guild would be watching closely? Would not such a dodge, introducing heretofore impermissible criteria, only invite greater condemnation? Moreover, such a maneuver might have been construed as a tacit capitulation to the critics' challenges, admitting that their accusations against Scripture were unanswerable. However, the tenor of their essay "Inspiration" conveys the opposite impression.

In their article Hodge and Warfield appeared confident and well-prepared to rebut many charges leveled against the inerrant quality of Scripture. And in point of fact, the original autograph idea was not crucial to their defense of Scripture. Their essay, "Inspiration," is about thirty-three pages in length. Of these thirty-three pages, about one half of one page is devoted to the original autograph idea. It is not discussed in isolation, but is inserted as part of a number of important qualifications established by the authors for conducting careful, critical analysis of the text. This procedure, much in accord with the practice of earlier nineteenth-century theologians, was but one of many guidelines they observed. It seems neither surprising nor sinister that they would enunciate such guidelines since criticism was rampant.

Though Sandeen insists that the Princetonians needed to resort to the missing documents in order to make their case, the contents of their essay provide a sharp rebuttal. The bulk of their work, which sounds much like that of earlier scholars, addresses questions of history, geography, and the internal harmony of Scripture. For example, maintaining Scripture's historical accuracy in everything it asserts, Hodge and Warfield wrote, "It was long boldly asserted that Luke was in error making Lysanias a contemporary tetrarch with the Herodian rulers. But it is now admitted that Josephus mentions an earlier and later Lysanius, and so corroborates Luke."[2] Apparent historical inaccuracies, when probed fully by the authors

2. Hodge and Warfield, "Inspiration," 247–48.

frequently proved unproblematic. The authors demonstrated this several times, offering reasonable explanations for a number of purported historical errors, sounding precisely like antebellum conservatives in the process.

Hodge and Warfield also pointed to geographical precision as another internal quality of Scripture arguing for its inerrancy. Contending that Scripture accurately identifies scores of countries, cities, and towns in the Near Eastern world, Hodge and Warfield observed:

> Between forty and fifty names of countries can be counted in the New Testament pages; every one is accurately named and placed. About the same number of foreign cities are named, and all equally accurately. Still more to the purpose, thirty-six Syrian and Palestinian towns are named, the great majority of which have been identified . . . this unvarying accuracy of statement is certainly consistent with the strictest doctrine of inspiration.[3]

Harmonizing apparently conflicting reports by the sacred writers is another way Hodge and Warfield confronted criticism. Authorial intent, they argued, just as many of their predecessors had, dictated the selection of various incidents to include or exclude from any narrative, reminding readers that omitting an event does not constitute a denial of it. Throughout their essay Hodge and Warfield addressed some of the most sophisticated criticism using actual data and logic to make their defense—just as the conservative elite had done before them.

Appealing to the autographs supposedly constructed an impregnable fortress around Scripture, insulating it from all assaults. But would such a maneuver really accomplish this goal? How far could it be pressed without creating chaos and confusion? Would the Princetonians, in their purported attempt to shield the Bible, have really argued that the original autographs differed substantially from the extant manuscripts? Exegetically, were the textual copies reliable reproductions of the originals? Did they represent biblical truth with a high degree of integrity? If so, the critics could still have at it. If not, the church was imperiled in all its doctrines. This brand of subterfuge would be irrelevant to the critics and unsettling to the orthodox. The cure would be more virulent than the disease.

Most textual critics believed that the documents contained the original readings, but that they existed in a shared form among the texts rather than as the exclusive property of any single text family. Since for most passages only a few possible renderings existed, a scholarly critic trained in the languages, could work through the exegetical issues involved. Therefore,

---

3. Ibid., 252.

this "dodge" could not insulate Scripture from attack. Indeed, it might restrain critics from making rash charges, but this is exactly in keeping with the purposes of Hodge and Warfield. Their recounting of the hermeneutic guidelines sounds much more like a summons to measured, careful analysis rather than an attempt to cancel all inquiry. Appeal to the original autographs would have been quite unable to defend Scripture in the way the critics suggest.

Furthermore, not all assaults against Scripture were subtle, some challenged large sections of text and textual themes such as the creation account, the reality of miracles, and the Mosaic authorship of the Pentateuch. With the critics waging war against such large biblical themes, it is difficult to imagine the supposed dodge deterring them. How would the original autograph theory protect the Bible from these kinds of slashing indictments? The assault against supernaturalism by secularization would seem to have called for more verve than demurely hiding behind missing documents. That amounts to trying to extinguish the Chicago fire with a squirt gun.

When analyzed from a number of angles, the original autograph criticism against the Princeton scholars fails to convince. The doctrine was clearly not new—it was at least as old as the century and very widespread. Its presence was not crucial to Hodge and Warfield's defense of inerrancy—they argued for the integrity of Scripture just as conservative scholars had done throughout the nineteenth-century. Nor could such a ploy insulate Scripture indefinitely from critical analysis. Rather than hermetically sealing Scripture off from all inquiry, the autograph doctrine invited careful, informed analysis of the text. Upon close inspection it seems clear that Hodge and Warfield sought to silence the critics of inerrancy in precisely the same manner as did their conservative predecessors.

Bibliography

Primary Sources

"Agreements and Differences Concerning the Bible." *Andover Review* 2 (1884) 79–82.

Alexander, Archibald. Review of *Woods on Inspiration*, by Leonard Woods. *Biblical Repertory and Theological Review* 3 (1831) 3–22.

———. *The Canon of the Old and New Testament Scriptures Ascertained: Or the Bible Complete Without the Apocrypha and Unwritten Traditions.* Philadelphia: Presbyterian Board of Publications, 1851.

———. *Evidences of the Authenticity, Inspiration and Canonical Authority of the Holy Scriptures.* Philadelphia: Presbyterian Board of Publications, 1837.

Bannerman, James. *Inspiration: The Infallible Truth and Divine Authority Of the Holy Scriptures.* T. & T. Clark, 1865.

Barrows, E. P. "The Alleged Disagreement between Paul and James." *Bibliotheca Sacra* 9 (1852) 761–82.

Beck, C. "Monogrammata Hermeneutices." *Biblical Repertory* 1 (1825) 27.

Berle, A. A. "The Bible as Authority and Index." *Bibliotheca Sacra* 51 (1894) 361–88.

Boardman, George N. "Inspiration; With Remarks on the Theory Presented in Ladd's Doctrine of Sacred Scripture." *Bibliotheca Sacra* 41 (1884) 506–49.

Briggs, Charles Augustus. *The Authority of Holy Scripture: An Inaugural Address.* New York: Scribner, 1891.

———. *Biblical Study: Its Principles, Methods, and History.* New York: Scribners, 1883.

———. *Whither? A Theological Question for the Times.* New York: Scribners, 1889.

Burr, E. F. "Infallible Scripture." *Bibliotheca Sacra* 44 (1887) 120–44.

Bushnell, Horace. *Christian Nurture.* New Haven: Yale University Press, 1888.

———. "Science and Religion." *Putnam's Magazine* 1 (1868) 272–74.

"A Call to Presbyterian Laymen." *Andover Review* 19 (1893) 193–98.

Cave, Alfred. "The Conflict between Religion and Science." *Andover Review* 14 (1890) 441–52.

Channing, William E. *A Selection from the Works of William E. Channing, D. D.* Boston: American Unitarian Association, 1865.

———. *The Works of William E. Channing.* 5 vols. Boston: Channing, 1849.

Collins, Charles Terry. "The Bible: A Gospel of Events." *Andover Review* 11 (1889) 46–62.

"The Conflict between Religion and Science." *Andover Review* (1890) 450–55.

"The Cosmogony of Genesis: Professor Driver's Critique of Professor Dana." *Bibliotheca Sacra* 45 (1888) 356–65.

"Current German Thought." *Andover Review* 7 (1887) 563–66.

Cutting, Sewall S. "Geology and Religion." *Christian Review* 15 (1850) 380–99.

Dale, R. W. "The Old Evangelicalism and the New." *Andover Review* 13 (1890) 430–34.

Dana, James D. "On the Cosmogony of Genesis." *Andover Review* 9 (1888) 197–200.

Dana, Jay J. "The Religion of Geology." *Bibliotheca Sacra* 10 (1853) 505–22.

The Defense of Professor Briggs before the Presbytery of New York. New York: Scribners, 1893.

Dick, John. *An Essay on the Inspiration of the Holy Scriptures of the Old and New Testaments.* Boston: Lincoln and Edwards, 1811.

———. *Lectures on Theology.* Philadelphia: Desilver, Thomas, and Company, 1836.

"Dr. Ladd on Alleged Discrepancies and Errors in the Bible." *Bibliotheca Sacra* 41 (1884) 389.

Driver, S. R. "Biblical and Historical Criticism: the Cosmogony of Genesis." *Andover Review* 8 (1887) 639–49.

Dyer, David. *The Plenary Inspiration of the Old and New Testaments.* Boston: Tappan, Whittemore, and Mason, 1849.

"Editorial." *Andover Review* 18 (1892) 300–305.

Edwards, B. B. "The Present State of Biblical Science." *Bibliotheca Sacra* 7 (1850) 1–13.

———. "Messianic Prophesies." *Bibliotheca Sacra* 9 (1852) 609–22.

Erdman, Charles R. "The Coming of Christ." In *The Fundamentals: A Testimony to the Truth,* 4:312, 1917. Reprint, Grand Rapids: Baker, 1996.

Fairchild, James H. "Authenticity and Inspiration of the Scriptures." *Bibliotheca Sacra* 49 (1892) 1–29.

Fitch, Eleazar T. "The True Doctrine of Inspiration." *Bibliotheca Sacra* 12 (1855) 217–63.

Foster, Frank. "The Argument from Christian Experience for the Inspiration of the Bible." *Bibliotheca Sacra* 40 (1883) 97–133.

Foster, Frank Hugh. "The Authority and Inspiration of the Scriptures." *Bibliotheca Sacra* 52 (1895) 69–96.

———. "The Authority and Inspiration of the Scriptures." *Bibliotheca Sacra* 52 (1895) 232–58.

Gardiner, Frederic. "The Bearing of Recent Scientific Thought upon Theology." *Bibliotheca Sacra* 35 (1878) 46–75.

———. "'Errors' of the Scriptures." *Bibliotheca Sacra* 36 (1879) 496–534.

Gaussen, S. R. L. "Interpretation of Scripture." *Princeton Review* 17 (1845) 409–28.

"Geographical Accuracy of the Bible." *Christian Review* 20 (1855) 451–69.

Gerhart, E. V. "Reformation Theology." *Andover Review* 3 (1885) 97–107.

———. "Reformation Theology." *Andover Review* 3 (1885) 211–27.

Gray, James M. "The Inspiration of the Bible—Definition, Extent, and Proof." In *The Fundamentals: A Testimony to the Truth,* 2:42–43, 1917. Reprint, Grand Rapids: Baker, 1996.

Haldane, Robert. *The Genuineness and Authenticity of the Holy Scriptures.* Edinburgh: Whyte, 1830.

Hascall, Jefferson. "Plenary Inspiration." *The Methodist Magazine and Quarterly Review* New Series 9 (1838) 156–66.

Hill, Thomas. "What is a Unitarian?" *Bibliotheca Sacra* 38 (1881) 25–47.

Hitchcock, Edward. "The Connection between Geology and the Mosaic History of Creation." *Biblical Repository* 5 (1835) 439–51.

———. "The Connection between Geology and the Mosaic History of Creation." *Biblical Repository* 6 (1835) 261–332.

———. "Remarks on Professor Stuart's Examination of Gen. 1 in Reference to Geology." *Biblical Repository* 7 (1836) 448–87.

———. "The Historical and Geological Deluges Compared." *Biblical Repository* 10 (1837) 328–74.

————. "The Historical and Geological Deluges Compared." *Biblical Repository* 11 (1838) 1–27.

————. "The Religion of Geology." *Bibliotheca Sacra* 17 (1860) 673–709.

Hitchcock, C. H. "The Relation of Geology to Theology." *Bibliotheca Sacra* 23 (1867) 363–88 and 429–81.

Hodge, Archibald Alexander. *Outlines of Theology: for Students and Laymen.* New York: Carter, 1860.

————. *Popular Lectures on Theological Themes.* Philadelphia: Presbyterian Board of Publication, 1887.

Hodge, A. A., and B. B. Warfield. "Inspiration." *Presbyterian Review* 6 (1881) 226–60.

Hodge, Charles. *What is Darwinism?* New York: Scribner, Armstrong, and Company, 1874.

————. *Systematic Theology.* 1873. Reprint, Grand Rapids: Eerdmans, 1981.

————. Review of *The Inspiration of Holy Scripture, its Nature and Proof,* by William Lee. *Princeton Review* 29 (1857) 660–98.

Hovey, Alvah. *Manual of Systematic Theology and Christian Ethics.* Philadelphia: American Baptist Publication Society, 1877.

"An Inconsistency and Useless Procedure: The Trial of Professor Briggs." *Andover Review* 15 (1891) 653–58.

"Inspiration of the Scriptures." *Freewill Baptist Quarterly* 3 (1855) 34–46.

"Is the Orthodox Pulpit Orthodox?" *Andover Review* 5 (1886) 517–24.

Johnson, F. H. "Reason and Revelation." *Andover Review* 5 (1886) 229–49.

Ladd, George T. *The Doctrine of Sacred Scripture.* 2 vols. Edinburgh: T. & T. Clark, 1883.

Langley, Alfred G. "Revelation, Inspiration, and Authority." *Andover Review* 15 (1891) 367–84.

Lee, William. *The Inspiration of the Holy Scriptures, Its Nature and Proof.* New York: Carter, 1857.

Lincoln, Heman. "Science not Supreme but Subordinate." *Bibliotheca Sacra* 42 (1885) 225–50.

Lord, Eleazar. *Inspiration not Guidance, nor Intuition or, the Plenary Inspiration Of the Holy Scriptures.* New York: Randolph, 1858.

————. *The Prophetic Office of Christ as Related to the Verbal Inspiration Of the Holy Scriptures.* New York: Anson and Randolph, 1859.

Lord, David N. ed. "The Inspiration of the Scriptures, Its Nature and Extent." *Theological and Literary Journal* 10 (1857) 1–45.

————. "The Two Records: The Mosaic and the Geological." *Theological and Literary Journal* 7 (1854–55) 129.

————. "On the Relation between the Holy Scriptures and Some Parts of Geological Science." *Theological and Literary Journal* 5 (1852–53) 588–612.

MacDill, David. *The Bible a Miracle; or the Word of God Its Own Witness: The Supernatural Inspiration of the Moral and Political Excellence.* Philadelphia: Rentoul, 1872.

McCook, John J. *The Appeal in the Briggs Heresy Case before the General Assembly of the Presbyterian Church in the United States of America.* New York: Rankin, 1893.

Moore, George F. "The Minister's Study of the Old Testament." *Andover Review* 12 (1889) 341–55.

————. Review of *The Divine Authority of the Bible,* by G. Frederick Wright. *Andover Review* 2 (1884) 613–17.

Moss, Lemuel. "Dr. Curtis on Inspiration." *Baptist Quarterly* 2 (1868) 83–117.

"The New York Presbytery and Professor Briggs." *Andover Review* 16 (1891) 511–15.

"On the Divine Authority of the Sacred Scriptures." *The Methodist Magazine* 2 (1819) 320–24.

"On the Relation between the Holy Scriptures and Some Parts of Geologic Science." *Theological and Literary Journal* 5 (1852–1853) 588–612.

Osgood, Harold. "Old Wine in Fresh Wineskins." *Bibliotheca Sacra* 50 (1893) 460–86.

Paine, J. A. "A Canonical Formula Introducing Certain Historical Books of the Old Testament." *Bibliotheca Sacra* 48 (1891) 652–59.

Park, Edwards A. "Remarks on the Biblical Repertory and Princeton Review." *Bibliotheca Sacra* (1851) 135–80.

Patton, Francis L. *The Inspiration of the Scriptures.* Philadelphia: Presbyterian Board of Publication, 1869.

"The Plenary Inspiration of the Scriptures." *Southern Presbyterian Review* 4 (1851) 457–98.

Pond, Enoch. Review of *The Inspiration of Holy Scripture, Its Nature and Proof,* by William Lee. *Bibliotheca Sacra* 15 (1858) 29–54.

———. "Alleged Discrepancies in the Bible." *Christian Review* 23 (1858) 380–415.

———. "The Interpretation of Scripture." *Theological and Literary Journal* 4 (1852) 415–25.

Porter, J. Leslie. "Miracles." *Bibliotheca Sacra* 30 (1873) 254–74.

"The Positive Side of Biblical Criticism." *Andover Review* 16 (1891) 172–75.

"Progressive Orthodoxy." *Andover Review* 4 (1885) 456–77.

"Proposed Changes Pertaining to Creed Subscription." *Andover Review* 11 (1889) 408–12.

Rawlinson, George. *The Historical Evidences of the Truth of the Scripture Records Stated Anew with Special Reference to the Doubts and Discoveries of Modern Times.* Boston: Gould and Lincoln, 1862.

"Rawlinson's Historical Evidences." *Christian Review* 25 (1860) 499–518.

"Religious Authority." *Andover Review* 17 (1892) 298–307.

"The Religious Beliefs of the Baptists." *Christian Review* 1 (1836) 514–31.

"The Religious Reason for Biblical Criticism." *Andover Review* 16 (1891) 403–6.

Review of *Lectures on the Inspiration of the Scriptures,* by Leonard Woods. *Christian Examiner* 8 (1830) 362–91.

Review of *Lectures on the Inspiration of the Scriptures,* by Leonard Woods. *Methodist Magazine and Quarterly Review* (1838) 356–67.

Rice, William North. "Twenty-Five Years of Scientific Progress." *Bibliotheca Sacra* 50 (1893) 1–29.

Sanday, William. *Inspiration: Eight Lectures on the Early History and Origin of the Doctrine of Biblical Inspiration.* London: Longmans, Green, and Company, 1893.

Schleiermacher, Friedrich. *The Life of Frederick Schleiermacher, as Unfolded in His Autobiography and Letters.* Translated by Frederica Rowan. London: Smith, Elder, 1859.

———. *Schleiermacher's Introductions to the Dialogues of Plato.* Translated by William Dobson. London: Cambridge, 1834.

Scott, H. M. "Notes of Delitzsch on True and False Defense of the Bible." *Bibliotheca Sacra* 48 (1891) 310–21.

Smith, Henry B. "The Inspiration of the Holy Scriptures: A Sermon Delivered before the Synod of New-York and New-Jersey in the First Presbyterian Church, Newark, N. J., October 17, 1855." New York: John A. Gray, 1855.

Smith, S. F. ed. "Inspiration of the Scriptures." *Christian Review* 12 (1847) 219–38.

Spring, Gardiner. "The Bible Not of Man: or the Argument for the Divine Origin of The Sacred Scriptures Drawn from the Scriptures Themselves." *Princeton Review* 20 (1848) 206–26.

Sterrett, J. Macbride. "Natural Realism; or Faith, the Basis of Science and Religion." *Bibliotheca Sacra* 31 (1874) 74–97.

Stowe, C. E. "The Right Interpretation of the Sacred Scriptures—the Helps and the Hindrances." *Bibliotheca Sacra* 10 (1853) 34–62.

———. "On Expository Preaching and the Principles Which Should Guide Us in the Exposition of Scripture." *Biblical Repository* 5 (1835) 384–402.

Stranger, A. (a fictitious name I presume). *The Trial of Dr. Briggs before the General Assembly.* New York: Randolph, 1893.

"Theological and Religious Intelligence: The Presbyterian Church in the United States of America against the Rev. Charles A. Briggs D. D." *Andover Review* 16 (1891) 529–42.

"Theological and Religious Intelligence: Response to the Charges and Specifications Submitted to the Presbytery of New York." *Andover Review* 16 (1891) 623–39.

"Theories of the Inspiration of the Scriptures." *American Presbyterian and Theological Review* 2 (1864) 312–51.

Torrey, Joseph, and D. D. Burlington. "Essay on Inspiration." *Bibliotheca Sacra* 15 (1858) 314–46.

"Tradition, Criticism, and Science." *Andover Review* 3 (1885) 47–53.

"The Trial of Presbyterianism." *Andover Review* 18 (1892) 90–92.

"The Two Records: The Mosaic and the Geological." *Theological and Literary Journal* 7 (1854–1855) 119–44.

Underhill, Edward Bean. "The Distinctive Features of the Baptist Denomination." *Christian Review* 17 (1852) 48–68.

Warfield, Benjamin B. "The Inspiration of the Bible." *Bibliotheca Sacra* 51 (1894) 614–40.

Warren, I. P. "The Inspiration of the Old Testament." *Bibliotheca Sacra* 41 (1884) 310–26.

Warring, Charles B. "Professor Huxley versus Genesis 1." *Bibliotheca Sacra* 49 (1892) 638–49.

Watson, Richard. *Theological Institutes: Or a View of the Evidences, Doctrines, Morals, and Institutions of Christianity.* New York: Bangs and Emory, 1825.

Westcott, B. F. *Introduction to the Study of the Gospels with Historical Explanatory Notes.* Boston: Gould and Lincoln, 1862.

Whedon, D. A. "Greek Text of the New Testament." *Methodist Quarterly Review* 9 (1868) 325–46.

Whitaker, William. *A Disputation on Holy Scripture.* Cambridge: Cambridge University Press, 1849.

Woods, Leonard. "The Inspiration of the Scriptures." *Christian Review* 9 (1844) 1–20.

———. *Lectures on the Inspiration of the Scriptures.* Andover: Flagg and Gould, 1829.

Wright, Frederick, et al. "Scripture or Logic—Which?" *Bibliotheca Sacra* 47 (1890) 669–81.

———. "Dr. Ladd on the Alleged Discrepancies and Errors of the Bible." *Bibliotheca Sacra* 41 (1884) 389–98.

Wright, Frederick G. "Dr Briggs's 'Whither?'" *Bibliotheca Sacra* 47 (1890) 136–53.

———. "The Affinity of Science for Christianity." *Bibliotheca Sacra* 46 (1889) 701–20.

———. "An Irenicon." *Bibliotheca Sacra* 52 (1895) 1–17.

Secondary Sources

Ahlstrom, Sydney E. *A Religious History of the American People.* New Haven: Yale University Press, 1972.

———, and Jonathan S. Carey. *An American Reformation: A Documentary History of Unitarian Christianity.* Connecticut: Wesleyan University Press, 1985.

Balmer, Randall H. "The Old Princeton Doctrine of Inspiration in the Context of Nineteenth-Century Theology: A Reappraisal." M.A. Thesis, Trinity Evangelical Divinity School, 1981.

Bannerman, James. *Fundamentalism*. London: SCM, 1977.

Barr, James. *The Scope and Authority of the Bible*. Philadelphia: Westminster, 1980.

Bowlby, John. *Charles Darwin: A New Life*. Norton, 1990.

Bowler, Peter J. *The Eclipse of Darwinism: Anti-Darwinian Evolution Theories in the Decades around 1900*. Baltimore: Johns Hopkins University Press, 1983.

———. *The Non-Darwinian Revolution: Reinterpreting a Historical Myth*. Baltimore: Johns Hopkins University Press, 1988.

———. *Evolution: The History of an Idea*. Berkeley: University of California Press, 1984.

Bozeman, Theodore Dwight. *Protestants in an Age of Science: The Baconian Ideal and Antebellum American Religious Thought*. Chapel Hill: University of North Carolina Press, 1977.

Brandt, Richard B. *The Philosophy of Schleiermacher: The Development of his Theory of Scientific and Religious Knowledge*. New York: Harper, 1941.

Coleridge, Samuel Taylor. *Confessions of an Inquiring Spirit*. 1841. Reprinted, Stanford: Stanford University Press, 1956.

Coxe, A. Cleveland, ed. *Ante-Nicene Fathers: The Writings of the Fathers down to A. D. 325*. 10 vols. Peabody, MA: Hendrickson, 1995.

Cross, F. L. ed. *The Oxford Dictionary of the Christian Church*. Oxford: Oxford University Press, 1974.

Cross, George. *The Theology of Schleiermacher: A Condensed Presentation of His Chief Work, "The Christian Faith."* Chicago: University of Chicago Press, 1911.

Dayton, Donald, and Robert K. Johnson eds. *The Variety of American Evangelicalism*. Downers Grove, IL: Intervarsity, 1991.

Emerton, Ephraim. *Unitarian Thought*. New York: MacMillian, 1916.

Ferm, Vergilius. *The Crisis in American Lutheran Theology: A Study of the Issue between American Lutheranism and Old Lutheranism*. New York: Century, 1927.

Foster, Frank Hugh. *A Genetic History of the New England Theology*. Chicago: University of Chicago Press, 1907.

Gonzalez, Justo L. *A History of Christian Thought*. 3 vols. Nashville: Abingdon, 1984.

Gunn, Roland Davis. "The Andover Case: A Study of the Role of Creeds in Nineteenth-Century Congregationalism." M. A. Thesis, Andover Newton Theological School, 1983.

Hatch, Nathan O., and Mark Noll eds. *The Bible in America: Essays in Cultural History*. New York: Oxford University Press, 1982.

Hutchison, William R. *The Modernist Impulse in American Protestantism*. Cambridge: Harvard University Press, 1976.

Lagerquist, L. D. *The Lutherans*. Westport, Connecticut: Greenwood, 1999.

Loetscher, Lefferts A. *The Broadening Church: A Study of Theological Issues in the Presbyterian Church since 1869*. Philadelphia: University of Pennsylvania Press, 1957.

Luccock, Halford E. and Paul Hutchinson. *The Story of Methodism*. New York: The Methodist Book Concern, 1926.

Lyttle, Charles H. *The Liberal Gospel as Set Forth in the Writings of William Ellery Channing*. Boston: Beacon, 1925.

Macintosh, H. R., and J. S. Stewart eds. *Friedrich Schleiermacher: The Christian Faith*. 2 vols. New York: Harper and Row, 1963.

Marsden, George M. *Fundamentalism and American Culture: The Shaping of Twentieth-Century Evangelicalism: 1870–1925.* New York: Oxford University Press, 1980.

———. *The Evangelical Mind and the New School Presbyterian Experience.* New Haven: Yale University Press, 1970.

———. *Reforming Fundamentalism: Fuller Seminary and the New Evangelicalism.* Grand Rapids: Eerdmans, 1987.

Mircea, Eliade, ed. *The Encyclopedia of Religion.* 16 vols. New York: Macmillan, 1987.

Muller, Richard A. *Dictionary of Latin and Greek Theological Terms Drawn Principally from Protestant Scholastic Theology.* Grand Rapids: Baker, 1985.

Nelson, John Oliver. "Charles Hodge: Nestor of Orthodoxy." In *The Lives of Eighteen from Princeton,* edited by William Thorpe, 192–211. Princeton: Princeton University Press, 1946.

Noll, Mark A. *A History of Christianity in the United States and Canada.* Grand Rapids: Eerdmans, 1992.

———. *Between Faith and Criticism: Evangelicals, Scholarship, and the Bible in America.* San Francisco: Harper and Row, 1986.

———. *The Scandal of the Evangelical Mind.* Grand Rapids: Eerdmans, 1994.

———. *Protestants in America.* Oxford: Oxford University Press, 2000.

Preus, Robert. *The Inspiration of Scripture: A Study of The Theology of the Seventeenth-Century Lutheran Dogmaticians.* Edinburgh: Oliver and Boyd, 1955.

Queens, Edward L., et al. *The Encyclopedia of American Religious History.* Boston: Proseworks, 1996.

Richey, Russell E. *Early American Methodism.* Bloomington, IN: Indiana University Press, 1991.

Robertson, A. T. *A Grammar of the Greek Testament in the Light of Historical Research.* Nashville: Broadman, 1934.

Rogers, Jack B. "The Church Doctrine of Biblical Authority." In *Biblical Authority,* edited by Jack Rogers, 15–46. Waco: Word, 1977.

Rogers, Jack B. and Donald K. McKim. *The Authority and Interpretation of the Bible: An Historical Approach.* San Francisco: Harper and Row, 1979.

Sandeen, Ernest R. *The Roots of Fundamentalism: British and American Millenarianism, 1800–1930.* Chicago: University of Chicago Press, 1970.

Satta, Ronald F. "Fundamentalism and Inerrancy: A Response to the Sandeen Challenge." *Evangelical Journal* 21 (2003) 66–80.

———. "The Case of Professor Charles A. Briggs: Inerrancy Affirmed." *Trinity Journal* 26 (2005) 69–90.

———. "Inerrancy: The Prevailing Orthodox Opinion of the Nineteenth-Century Theological Elite." *Faith and Mission Journal* 24 (2007) 79–96.

Schaff, Philip. *The Creeds of Christendom: with a History and Critical Notes.* 3 vols. Grand Rapids: Baker, 1983.

Semmel, Bernard. *The Methodist Revolution.* New York: Basic, 1973.

Trembath, Kern Robert. *Evangelical Theories of Biblical Inspiration.* New York: Oxford University Press, 1987.

Vanderpool, Harold Young. "The Andover Conservatives: Apologetics, Biblical Criticism, and Theological Change at Andover Theological Seminary, 1808–1880." Ph.D. diss., Harvard University, 1971.

Walker, Williston. *Ten New England Leaders.* New York: Silver, Burdett, 1901.

Weber, Timothy. "The Two-Edged Sword: The Fundamentalist use of the Bible." In *The Bible in America: Essays in Cultural History,* edited by Nathan Hatch and Mark Noll, 101–20. New York: Oxford: Oxford University Press, 1982.

Wells, David F. ed. *Reformed Theology in America: A History of its Modern Development.* Grand Rapids: Eerdmans, 1985.

Wilbur, Earl Morse. *A History of Unitarianism: in Transylvania, England, and America.* Cambridge: Harvard University Press, 1952.

William, Gordon R. (Chairman of the Resource Committee). *The National Union Catalogue.* London: Mansell, 1974.

Woodbridge, John D., and Randall H. Balmer. "The Princetonians and Biblical Authority: An Assessment of the Ernest Sandeen Proposal." In *Scripture And Truth,* edited by D. A. Carson and John D. Woodbridge, 251–79. Grand Rapids: Baker, 1994.

Young, William T. *The Congregationalists.* New York: Greenwood, 1990.